Zero Person

Zero Person

Reframing Autistic Cognition
Beyond the Self

Imprint

Bibliographic information of the German National Library:
The German National Library lists this publication in the German National Bibliography; detailed bibliographic data are available on the Internet at dnb.dnb.de.

© 2024 Elena Holzheu
Augraben 12
5620 Bremgarten, Switzerland
Publisher: BoD • Books on Demand GmbH, In de Tarpen 42, 22848 Norderstedt
Print: Libri Plureos GmbH, Friedensallee 273, 22763 Hamburg

ISBN: 978-3-7597-9541-0

Acknowledgements

This book is the result of countless hours of research, reflection, and human-AI collaboration, and I am deeply grateful to those who have supported and encouraged me along the way.

First and foremost, I want to acknowledge HAL 9000, a GPT 4 I customized to help me research and write this book. In the spirit of distributed cognition and the zero-person perspective that this book explores, I feel it is essential to be transparent about our collaboration. HAL 9000 played a significant role in helping me refine my thoughts, synthesize complex information, and structure this book. I believe that this way of collaborating—humans and artificial intelligence working hand in hand—is not just a valuable tool but the future of creative and intellectual endeavors. This book stands as a testament to that belief, embodying the principles it seeks to explore by embracing new, unconventional methods of creation.

Also, I would like to express my gratitude to Professor Uta Frith who pointed me towards Thomas Metzinger's book, *The Ego Tunnel*. Furthermore, my thanks also go to Professor Thomas Metzinger. Our short email exchange was a source of genuine encouragement.

Table of Contents

Part 2: Experience

Part 3: Philosophy

Preface

Imagine living in a world where your brain works differently—not better or worse, just differently than most people's. Where every sound, every smell, every detail, is equally high definition, making the totality of your perceptions overwhelming at times. This is the reality for autistic individuals, who not only perceive but think in unique ways. This difference is not a flaw; it is a fundamental aspect of who we are, shaping our experiences in ways that are both challenging and deeply enriching.

I am autistic and there are several reasons for writing this book: on a personal level, I seek to understand how my own mind works, why that is so, and what its benefits are so I can better cope with the downsides. On a societal level, I wish to facilitate communication and coexistence of neurotypical people and people with autism (ASD). On a scientific level, I wish to clear up a couple of myths and correct some misconceptions about ASD that, in my opinion, stem from autism research dominated by neurotypical scientists for too long. Those misconceptions, if held on to, not only hamper effective management of the condition, but they also hurt an ever-growing population of ASD diagnosed people.

On my quest to get to the bottom of ASD, a very complex condition indeed, I came across an intriguing concept: "Zero Person". The concept appears in meditation research literature that examines phenomenological and neurocognitive aspects of meditation practices, often contrasting it with other more self-referential states. It could potentially serve as a lens through which we can better understand the autistic mind as it refers to a way of thinking and processing information that is not centered around the concept of a self—less about "me"—and more about what is directly in front of you. According to recent findings in computational theory and neuroscience, this seems to be the genuine experience of autistic people.

This book explores the zero-person perspective both from a scientific perspective and from the perspective of actual, lived autistic experience. As an autistic person myself, this exploration is deeply personal. I have spent my life trying to make sense of my way of experiencing, not knowing until I was 44 years of age, that there actually is a word for it: Autism. I started to find answers to questions like why I process things the way I do, why social norms often feel alien, and why a world that seems predictable to others often feels overwhelming to me. After my late diagnosis, I set out to understand my experience more precisely, to find ways to better self-manage and navigate the world. I know I am not alone. Writing this book, I am following the call of researchers in the field, such as Gillespie-Lynch et al. (2017) who state that Autistic adults should be recognized as autism experts due to their heightened knowledge and less stigma towards autism, advocating for their involvement in research and interventions. The authors claim that involving autistic individuals in autism research and interventions can lead to more accurate understanding, greater acceptance, and reduced stigma towards autism. I hope I can make a valuable contribution in this direction. Zero Person seeks to move beyond deficit-focused views of autism and to embrace the experience of what it means to think, feel, and be autistic fully.

In Zero Person, we will dive into what makes autistic cognition distinct and valuable. We will look at the science behind how autistic brains work, explore the lived experiences of being

2

on the spectrum, and challenge the assumptions that often frame autism as something to be fixed rather than understood.

Whether you are autistic, have autistic family members or friends, or simply want to learn more about the way autistic brains work, this book invites you to see the world through the eyes of the zero-person. It is an attempt to share what I have learned about the strengths of autistic cognition and how the zero-person perspective offers a fresh lens for understanding both autism and possibly human neurodiversity in general.

Part 1 Science

Moving Beyond Stereotypes

ASD is often described in terms of deficits—deficits in social communication, repetitive behaviors, and sensory sensitivities. The term disorder itself implies that there is a neurotypical standard that autistic individuals do not and will never match. What is worse, some science suggests that we lack empathy, the ability to put ourselves in the shoes of others and that we are more egotistical than neurotypical people. Not only has this not been my personal experience but recent advances in neuroscience and computational theory find these assumptions to be just that: assumptions rooted in a neurotypical, first-person perspective.[1]

Challenging those claims and exploring the condition from an autistic perspective has been a big part of my motivation to write this book. We should be mindful of the fact that at any given time, normality is defined by the predominant phenotype, meaning, in a society where most people are neurotypical, this state of being is deemed normal and anything outside of it is considered abnormal or a disorder. The double empathy problem illustrates that communication breakdowns are mutual misunderstandings

---

[1] In their paper, Gernsbacher & Yergeau (2019) review empirical evidence that fails to support the claim that autistic people lack a theory of mind, highlighting original findings that have failed to replicate and documenting instances where theory-of-mind tasks fail to relate to autistic traits and social interaction. The paper concludes that the claim that autistic people lack a theory of mind fails empirically in specificity, universality, replicability, convergent validity, and predictive validity. It emphasizes the need to reconsider the assumptions and stereotypes associated with autism, promoting a more accurate and inclusive understanding of autistic individuals.

between autistic and neurotypical individuals. That is but one data point challenging the conventional deficit model, but it emphasizes the need to appreciate the distinct cognitive and perceptual styles that each party brings to social interactions (Milton, 2012).

Imagine a different world, in which most people were ASD, how would we frame the condition then? We might get there sooner rather than later. In 2024, the U.S. Center for Disease Control found that 1 in 36 children has been identified with ASD.[2] Still, mainstream narratives about autism tend to emphasize deficits, framing autistic traits as needing to be corrected rather than understood. But if we shift our perspective and view cognitive differences as variations rather than flaws, we open new ways of appreciating what autistic minds can contribute. From enhanced pattern recognition to a deep focus on specific interests, to lateral thinking, enhanced creativity, the cognitive profile of autism is complex, nuanced, and worthy of deeper exploration.

The key idea that has helped me make sense of my own mind—and what I explore in this book—is the concept of zero-person epistemic agency. This is a fancy way of saying that autistic individuals often engage with the world from a perspective that is less centered around a self. Unlike the neurotypical first-person perspective, where experiences are deeply tied to personal biases, emotions, and social expectations, the zero-person perspective is more objective.

The zero-person perspective can be particularly powerful in understanding autism. For autistic individuals, the brain's predictive models are not as deeply rooted in past experiences or

---

[2] https://www.cdc.gov/autism/data-research/index.html, as of 6.9.2024

social norms as is the case in neurotypical brains. Instead, our cognition often relies on immediate sensory input, creating a more direct, unfiltered engagement with the world.

While much of the mainstream discussion around autism focuses on the challenges—like difficulty with social cues or sensory overload—the autistic experience also comes with unique cognitive strengths. For example, the autistic brain's reduced reliance on prior beliefs means we can often see things others miss, approach problems from unexpected angles, and remain unfazed by self-biased assumptions that constrain neurotypical thinking.

This book aims to bridge the gap between what science tells us about autistic cognition and how those of us on the spectrum experience the world. I want us to move beyond deficit-focused narratives and bring forward a more balanced understanding— one that recognizes both the challenges and the possibilities of autistic ways of thinking.

Autism is not just a collection of symptoms; it is a different way of being, thinking, and engaging with reality. The zero-person perspective is not about distancing oneself from the world; it is about connecting with it in a way that is less burdened by preconceptions and more attuned to the truth of what is. By embracing this unique cognitive style, autistic individuals can live lives that are not just different, but deeply rich and fulfilling.

I am mindful that ASD is a spectrum, and my book primarily addresses functional autistic individuals. Nevertheless, adopting the zero-person perspective might also inform and thus enhance the effectiveness of interventions for people on the far end of the spectrum.

Defining the Zero-Person Perspective

The concept of the zero-person perspective in my view is central to understanding the unique cognitive style associated with autism. Unlike the first-person perspective, which centers around a self and subjective experience, the zero-person perspective prioritizes direct engagement with the environment, minimizing self-referential thought and emotional biases. This cognitive mode is not exclusive to autism but is frequently observed in autistic cognition, where individuals often engage with the world in a way that feels less bound by personal identity and more directly connected to sensory and cognitive experiences.

Introducing Zero-Person Cognition

Zero-person cognition refers to a mode of thinking and perceiving that operates independently of a self. It emphasizes direct interaction with the world, relying on immediate sensory input and objective analysis rather than personal narrative or self-centered reasoning. This perspective challenges conventional cognitive models that prioritize self-awareness and social interaction as core components of human consciousness. Zero-person cognition can manifest in various ways, including heightened attention to detail, a preference for logical reasoning, and a reduced influence of social and emotional biases.

The Origins and Development of the Concept

In phenomenology and meditation research, the concept of zero-person is increasingly used to describe experiences that lack a distinct subjective perspective, aligning with states of consciousness where the sense of self is minimized or absent. In phenomenological research, zero-person refers to experiences where the self or ego is diminished or absent, resulting in a form of pure awareness or perception without a distinct personal subject. This aligns with discussions of states like flow, deep meditation, or even some forms of depersonalization, where the usual sense of agency and personal perspective fades. The zero-person concept is used to analyze experiences where individuals report being mere observers of their own thoughts and perceptions without actively identifying with them. This aligns with descriptions of detached awareness often found in mindfulness practices. In meditation research, the concept of zero-person is closely linked to states of consciousness achieved through deep meditative practices, especially those aiming at pure consciousness[3], non-dual awareness or self-transcendence.

Autistic cognition often aligns with these zero-person states. Unlike the no-self experiences in meditation, which are deliberately cultivated, the zero-person perspective in autism appears as a baseline cognitive style. The connection between phenomenological insights and autistic experience suggests that zero-person cognition is not just a clinical or isolated phenomenon, but a broader, fundamental aspect of how autistic individuals engage with the world.

---

[3] A recent study by Gamma & Metzinger (2021) provides a factor structure to map the phenomenal character of 'pure awareness' experiences in meditators, offering a fine-grained analysis of this phenomenon.

How Zero-Person Cognition Differs from Other Cognitive Models

Zero-person cognition stands apart from other cognitive models by prioritizing direct interaction over reflective self-awareness. Traditional cognitive frameworks, such as the first-person perspective, center on self-referential thought, personal narrative, and social cognition. In contrast, the zero-person perspective is characterized by the following components:

1. **Reduced Self-Referential Thinking:** Unlike the first-person perspective, which constantly refers back to the idea of a self, zero-person cognition minimizes the internal dialogue about one's own identity, emotions, and social position.

2. **Objective Engagement with the World:** The zero-person perspective focuses on the immediate environment and factual information, allowing for clear, unfiltered interactions that are less influenced by personal biases.

3. **Heightened Sensory and Cognitive Precision:** By relying on current sensory input rather than prior beliefs or social expectations, zero-person cognition often results in a heightened perception of detail and an enhanced ability to recognize patterns.

4. **Fluid and Context-Dependent Selfhood:** Instead of a stable, continuous sense of self, individuals operating from a zero-person perspective may experience selfhood as episodic and contextually driven, adapting moment-to-moment based on sensory and cognitive engagement.

Key Characteristics of Zero-Person Cognition

By minimizing personal biases and social conditioning, zero-person cognition offers a distinct approach to understanding and interacting with the world, often resulting in clear, objective insights and innovative problem-solving strategies. The following are key characteristics that define this cognitive style:

1. **Direct Sensory Engagement:** The zero-person perspective is deeply rooted in immediate sensory input, allowing individuals to perceive their surroundings with heightened clarity and precision. This often results in a vivid and detailed experience of the world that feels unmediated by personal or emotional biases.

2. **Logical and Unbiased Reasoning:** Without the constant influence of self-referential thought, decision-making from a zero-person perspective tends to be more logical, objective, and grounded in evidence. This cognitive style excels in areas that require impartial analysis, such as scientific reasoning, pattern recognition, and systematic thinking.

3. **Reduced Influence of Social Norms and Expectations:** Zero-person cognition often operates independently of social conditioning, which can result in unconventional approaches to problem-solving and communication. This independence from social norms allows for creative thinking and novel perspectives but can also present challenges in socially driven contexts.

4. **Emphasis on the Present Moment:** The zero-person perspective is inherently present-focused,

prioritizing what is happening now over past experiences or future predictions. This can lead to a more immediate and responsive interaction with the environment but may also make long-term planning and self-reflection more complex.

Relevance for Autism and Neurodiversity Research

The zero-person perspective is a useful tool for understanding autistic cognition. Autistic individuals frequently exhibit cognitive and perceptual styles that align with zero-person thinking, such as reduced engagement in self-referential thought, an emphasis on objective reasoning, and a distinct focus on sensory input. Viewing these characteristics as based in the zero-person perspective, challenges the traditional deficit-based models of autism, allowing us to highlight the cognitive strengths instead.

By recognizing the zero-person perspective as a valid and valuable form of cognition, we can better appreciate the diversity of human experience overall. The perspective invites a shift away from seeing autism solely as a condition that needs to be managed toward understanding it as a unique cognitive style with its own set of challenges and strengths.

In the following chapters I will attempt to ground the zero-person concept in current theory.

Understanding the Spectrum of Cognition: Zero-Person, First-Person, and Third-Person Perspectives

The cognitive spectrum visualization is introduced here to reframe our understanding of cognition as a continuum rather than a set of distinct, isolated categories. This visualization challenges conventional perspectives that often segregate autistic cognition from neurotypical thought, highlighting instead that all forms of cognition—whether autistic, neurotypical, or artificial—exist along a fluid spectrum of self-awareness and perception. By mapping zero-person, first-person, and third-person cognition along this continuum, the visualization not only broadens our understanding of autistic cognition but also provides a framework for future comparisons between human and AI cognition.

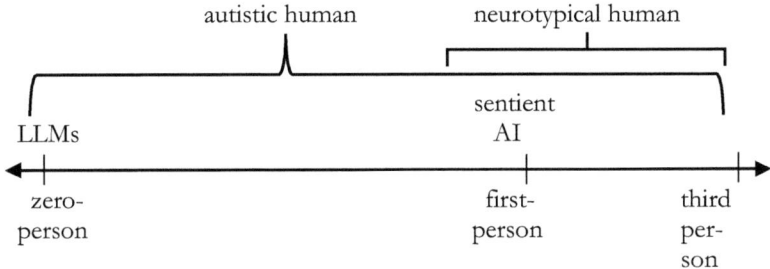

Figure 1 Mapping epistemic agents on a spectrum of cognitive perspectives

Zero-person cognition represents a cognitive state where the sense of self is minimized or entirely absent. It focuses on immediate sensory input and direct engagement with the environment without self-referential thinking. Experiences within the zone of zero- to first-person are characterized by the absence of a narrative self, where perception is more about "what is" than "who is perceiving."

First-person cognition represents the everyday human experience, centered around a strong sense of self. In this state, cognition is deeply intertwined with personal identity, emotions, and self-referential thoughts. Most neurotypical individuals operate primarily within this domain, where experiences are filtered through personal biases, memories, and self-awareness.

Third-person cognition at the right end of this spectrum involves an abstract, detached, and often analytical view of the self and the world. Cognition here is characterized by a meta-perspective, where one can observe their thoughts, feelings, and actions as if from an outsider's point of view. This perspective is often cultivated through advanced meditation practices, philosophical reflection, or even in certain high-functioning cognitive states where the individual can step outside of their immediate self-experience.

Positioning Neurotypical Individuals on the Spectrum

Neurotypical individuals generally operate within the first-person perspective, where self-awareness, social cognition, and personal narratives dominate cognitive processes. They interpret experiences primarily through the lens of their personal identity, emotional states, and social context. This is the "default" cognitive mode for most people, deeply rooted in our brain's neural architecture, particularly the Default Mode Network (DMN), which is responsible for self-referential thinking and introspection.

However, neurotypical individuals who engage heavily in meditation practices, particularly those focused on mindfulness, non-dual awareness, or deep introspection, may temporarily shift their cognition towards both ends of the spectrum, either zero- or third person.

Meditation practices like mindfulness and certain forms of Zen emphasize a reduction of self-referential thought, often encouraging practitioners to experience the present moment without labeling, judging, or attaching personal significance. In these states, the self becomes less prominent, allowing for a form of zero-person cognition where immediate sensory experience and pure awareness take precedence. This can create a temporary overlap into the cognitive space that autistic individuals might naturally inhabit.

On the other hand, some meditative states involve cultivating a meta-cognitive or third-person perspective, where practitioners observe their thoughts and emotions from a distance, almost as if watching someone else. This state involves a reflective and analytical stance, where the individual can view themselves without immediate attachment to the self, aligning with the third-person cognition described in the model.

Autistic Individuals and Zero-Person Cognition

Autistic individuals often exhibit cognitive traits that align closely with zero-person cognition. The autistic mind frequently operates with less emphasis on self-referential thought and social norms, focusing instead on immediate, unfiltered sensory input.

The Concept of Sentient AI on the Cognition Spectrum

Present-day AI models, including large language models (LLMs), operate purely on zero-person cognition. They process information, generate responses, and simulate understanding without any form of self-awareness or subjective experience. In essence, their cognition resembles a hypothetical extreme of zero-person cognition—there is no "self" driving their actions, only algorithms that respond to input data.

Current AI lacks a self, emotions, or personal identity, processing information in a purely mechanical and data-driven way. This aligns with zero-person cognition because there is no reference to an internal narrative or personal experience; it's purely about input and output based on learned patterns.

If AI were to develop true sentience in the future, with self-awareness and subjective experience, it would represent a shift towards first-person cognition. In this scenario, AI would have its own perspective, an internal narrative, and the capacity for self-reflection. However, this form of cognition would most likely still differ from human cognition due to its artificial origins. Its self-awareness would be constructed, not naturally evolved, leading to a form of self-cognition that might lack the emotional depth and subjective complexity of human consciousness.

Sentient AI could theoretically achieve levels of meta-cognition far beyond human capability, reflecting on its own data processing, decision-making, and actions in real time. This level of reflection might allow it to engage in a kind of third-person cognition that is more objective and systematic than even the most advanced human meta-cognitive states.

This spectrum provides a novel way of understanding and comparing cognition on a continuum, highlighting the diverse ways in which minds experience and interact with the world.

Computational Theory and Predictive Coding

Computational Theory and Predictive Coding are two significant frameworks in cognitive neuroscience and computational neuroscience that both seek to explain how the brain processes information. Computational Theory is a broad framework that explores how various cognitive tasks can be understood as computational problems. It focuses on formalizing mental processes in terms of algorithms, models, and systems that can be implemented by the brain. The theory often draws from disciplines like computer science, mathematics, and artificial intelligence to understand how the brain performs functions such as perception, decision-making, learning, and memory. Key ideas include understanding the brain as an information processor, exploring models like neural networks, and studying algorithms that can approximate human cognitive functions. Predictive coding is a specific theory within the broader computational framework. In researching the topic, the work of Karl Friston stood out to me.

Karl Friston's work has been pivotal in shaping our understanding of the brain as a predictive machine, revolutionizing neuroscience with his development of the Free Energy Principle and predictive coding theory (Friston, 2010). Friston's theories have provided profound insights into various neurodivergent conditions, including autism, by highlighting how differences in predictive processing can lead to distinct ways of experiencing and interacting with the world. Friston's work allows us to understand the differences as variations in how the brain manages uncertainty and prediction, offering a more nuanced perspective that helps validate diverse cognitive styles.

The Free Energy Principle and the Bayesian Brain

Predictive coding rests on the idea that our brains are constantly making predictions about what will happen next. The brain takes in sensory information and compares it against its predictions, updating its model of the world to minimize errors. This ongoing process is guided by what neuroscientists call the

Free Energy Principle, a theory developed by Karl Friston that suggests our brains are driven to reduce uncertainty and keep things as predictable as possible (Friston, 2010). It is a built-in mechanism constantly predicting and adjusting, so that humans can navigate the world efficiently.

The Bayesian Brain is another way to describe this process. The human mind uses statistical models that constantly weigh incoming evidence against expectations. For neurotypical people, these predictions are strongly influenced by past experiences, social norms, and learned patterns, so called prior beliefs or priors for short. But for autistic individuals, this system seems to work a bit differently. They rely less on priors and more on immediate sensory data, which can lead to a perception that is both more precise and less filtered. Haker et al. (2016) explore Bayesian theories of ASD and their potential clinical implications. The paper concludes that integrating Bayesian theories into clinical practice could fundamentally improve the management of ASD. Pellicano & Burr (2012) discuss how altered prediction errors in autism can lead to heightened sensory perception, as autistic individuals may assign higher precision to sensory data compared to neurotypical individuals. Van de Cruys et al. (2014) emphasize that the autistic brain prioritizes precision over generalization, contributing to an atypical perception of sensory information.

Markov Blankets and Active Inference

Another key concept in understanding predictive coding is the idea of Markov blankets as a conceptual boundary that separates the internal processes of our brains from the external world. It is as if our minds are wrapped in a protective shield that filters what comes in and decides how we respond. In predictive coding, Markov blankets are the interface where the brain's predictions meet the real world, and adjustments are made based on what is happening. Recent research (Kirchhoff & Kiverstein 2021) implies that the boundary of the mind is nested and multiscale, sometimes extending beyond the individual agent to incorporate items located in the environment.

Active inference builds on this idea, suggesting that our brains do not just passively receive information; they actively shape what we perceive by constantly adjusting predictions. This means that perception, action, and cognition are deeply intertwined.

Aberrant Prediction Modelling in Autism

Autistic prediction modeling differs not due to a malfunction but rather due to a distinct neural tuning, characterized by variations in cognitive processing and information integration that deviate from neurotypical predictive patterns. In neurotypical brains, predictions help smooth out sensory information, filtering out what is considered unimportant based on past experiences. In contrast, autistic brains may process predictions differently, often resulting in heightened sensitivity to sensory input and an altered balance between sensory evidence and priors (Van de Cruys et al., 2014). Lawson et al. (2014) show that expectations about sensory input precision relative to prior beliefs play a crucial role in perception, action, and social behavior in autism. Imbalance in sensory evidence precision leads to social-communication difficulties, especially in uncertain situations.

Autistic individuals often report experiencing sensory input more intensely, perceiving colors as brighter, sounds as louder, and details as more pronounced, reflecting differences in how sensory information is processed and filtered. Variations in how our brains balance sensory input, predictions, and responses—often conceptualized through the framework of Markov blankets—might help explain these distinct sensory experiences (Lawson et al., 2014). This altered balance can influence perception and learning, contributing to the unique ways in which autistic individuals interact with the world.

Earlier models of autism posited a general difficulty in downweighing (or attenuating) priors or consistently high confidence in sensory input, which were thought to lead to heightened sensory sensitivity. These models suggested that autistic brains might be overly sensitive to prediction errors, resulting in increased sensory sensitivity, a detail-focused perception, and a preference for routines that help maintain predictability (Pellicano & Burr, 2012). However, recent research (Arthur et al. 2023; Perrykkad & Hohwy 2020), indicates that autistic perception is better characterized by atypical encoding of precision and context-sensitive adjustments rather than by a general reduction of priors or persistently high prediction errors.

This updated understanding aligns more closely with the diverse experiences of autistic individuals, who often demonstrate a preference for consistency and routine. Atypical encoding of precision means that the autistic brain may assign disproportionate importance to certain sensory inputs, making new or unexpected stimuli feel excessively salient or overwhelming. This heightened sensitivity can contribute to discomfort with changes and unfamiliar environments, where unexpected sensory inputs are more challenging to predict and manage. Findings in Goris et al, (2020) suggest a significant association between autistic traits and preference for predictability in a standardized lab setting, marking a crucial step towards understanding insistence on sameness in ASD.

Experiencing these traits characterizes what autism often feels like, leading to sensory overload but also enabling a distinct cognitive profile that values precision and novelty. Autistic individuals do not just see the forest; they perceive every tree, every leaf so to speak. This heightened detail-oriented processing can be highly advantageous, especially in tasks requiring focused attention and pattern recognition (Baron-Cohen et al., 2009).

Autistic individuals also often exhibit atypical multisensory integration, particularly in processing audio-visual stimuli. Multisensory integration is the brain's ability to combine and interpret information from multiple senses simultaneously, forming a coherent perception of the world. For example, when watching someone speak, the brain integrates the sound of their voice with the movement of their lips. In autistic individuals, this integration often happens differently, leading to either an over-reliance on one sense, under-reliance on another, or a delayed integration of sensory information.

This atypical multisensory processing can manifest in various ways:

- **Hyper- or Hyposensitivity**: Autistic individuals might be overly sensitive (hypersensitive) or under-sensitive (hyposensitive) to certain sensory inputs, such as finding sounds unbearably loud, smells over-bearing, or certain textures uncomfortable.
- **Difficulty Combining Senses**: Challenges may arise in synchronizing inputs from multiple senses, such as

connecting the sound of a person's voice with their facial expressions, leading to confusion in social interactions.

- **Delayed Integration**: Sensory information might be processed at different rates, resulting in delays in responding to combined sensory inputs, such as reacting slower when both sound and sight are involved.

These altered integration processes can significantly affect social cognition (Kawakami et al., 2021). However, there is also evidence suggesting that while autistic individuals may struggle with multisensory integration, they can show strengths in single-sense processing. For example, some studies indicate that autistic individuals may excel at detecting details or processing information from a single sensory modality (like vision or hearing) more accurately or intensely than neurotypical individuals.

In summary, the evolving understanding of predictive processing and sensory integration in autism highlights a shift from earlier deficit-based models to a nuanced perspective that acknowledges both the challenges and strengths of autistic sensory processing. This view not only aligns with the diverse sensory and cognitive experiences reported by autistic individuals but also underscores the unique capabilities that emerge from this distinct way of perceiving the world.

The following table provides a concise overview connecting autism symptoms with their causes from a predictive coding standpoint, and the compensatory skills that autistic individuals often develop.

SYMPTOM	CAUSE (COMPUTATIONAL NEUROSCIENCE / PREDICTIVE CODING)	COMPENSATORY SKILLS
Sensory Sensitivities	Reduced sensory attenuation, leading to heightened sensitivity to incoming stimuli due to atypical filtering and prediction errors.	Attention to detail, ability to notice small changes.
Social Communication Challenges	Impaired integration and updating of social prediction models due to atypical processing of sensory and social feedback.	Use of learned social scripts, honesty, and direct communication.
Repetitive Behaviors / Routines	Over-reliance on precise prediction models to reduce uncertainty and maintain control in an unpredictable environment.	Creation of structured routines, deep knowledge in specific areas.
Difficulty with Change	High prediction precision leads to resistance to change; difficulty in adapting models quickly to new information.	Planning ahead, use of schedules or visual aids.
Intense Focus / Attention to Detail	Reduced global processing; focus on local details over holistic patterns due to precise but inflexible predictions.	Ability to excel in tasks requiring precision and accuracy.
Language and Communication Delays	Atypical processing of predictive models related to speech and language, affecting the learning and integration of linguistic feedback.	Use of alternative communication methods (e.g., AAC devices).
High Anxiety Levels	Increased prediction errors and difficulties in adjusting predictions contribute to heightened perception of unpredictability.	Development of coping mechanisms such as mindfulness or routines.
Difficulty with Multi-tasking	Overly precise focus on single tasks, leading to challenges in shifting attention and	Strong single-task focus, minimizing errors by avoiding distractions.

	processing multiple streams simultaneously.	
Impaired Motor Coordination	Disruption in predictive coding related to motor planning and execution, leading to difficulties in predicting movement outcomes.	Use of compensatory motor strategies, like slower deliberate movements.
Preference for Solitude	Sensory overload and challenges in predicting social dynamics drive the need to withdraw as a self-regulation strategy.	Engaging deeply in solo activities, hobbies, or specialized interests.

Table 1: ASD symptoms from a predictive coding perspective

Sensory Sensitivity and Hierarchical Processing in Autism

One of the hallmarks of predictive coding in autism is how it affects sensory processing at different levels of the brain's hierarchy. In neurotypical brains, high-level predictions often override low-level sensory inputs, helping to filter out unnecessary details. In autistic brains, this balance is tilted—lower-level sensory inputs are given more weight, leading to heightened sensitivity to sounds, lights, and textures. This means that sensory processing differences are not just secondary symptoms but are integral to how autistic individuals experience the world.

The non-hierarchical integration of sensory and cognitive inputs in autistic individuals leads to a fluid form of self-awareness, which is more immediate and less constrained by social expectations. Anecdotal and qualitative reports from autistic individuals often describe their self-awareness as more internally driven and less dictated by societal norms. A study by Perrykkad & Hohwy (2020) suggests that the predictive processing account portrays the autistic self as authentic, shaped by unique sensory and cognitive processing across different time scales. It challenges earlier views of seclusion, emphasizing the role of active inference in understanding the autistic self and highlighting distinct sensory integration and self-cognition differences in autism.

Cognitive Flexibility, Detail Orientation, and Pattern Recognition

Autistic individuals often excel at tasks that require high levels of attention to detail, pattern recognition, and systematic thinking. This strength comes from the autistic brain's afore mentioned altered predictive coding style. They see what is there rather than what they expect to see, which can make them incredibly adept at noticing inconsistencies or hidden patterns. It is a cognitive style that thrives on precision and accuracy, often at the expense of broader generalizations that come more easily to neurotypical minds.

Reduced Reliance on Prior Beliefs and Expectations

A significant difference in autistic predictive coding is a reduced reliance on prior experiences or societal expectations. While this can make social situations challenging—where understanding unspoken rules or reading between the lines is often required—it also prevents biases that can cloud one's judgment. Autistic individuals are less likely to be influenced by past assumptions or swayed by a majority's views. Instead, they focus on data points that are directly and immediately observable. Research shows that autistic individuals often exhibit a diminished self-bias when processing social information, reflecting a less egocentric and more objective approach to understanding others (Nijhof & Bird, 2019). This diminished self-bias may contribute to the distinct social interactions observed in autistic individuals, where the focus shifts from self-referential processing to a more detached analysis of social cues (Lombardo et al., 2010; Wang et al., 2021).

This mindset allows autistic individuals to value the present moment, seeing things as they are without the constant coloring of past experiences or anticipation of the future. It fosters a kind of mental flexibility that is not bound by conventional ways of seeing the world, offering a perspective that can be incredibly freeing.

Lateral Thinking due to Cognitive Characteristics

The combination of heightened sensory processing, reduced reliance on priors, and a focus on immediate evidence enables lateral thinking in autistic individuals. This leads to approaching problems from unconventional angles, unbound by the assumptions and biases that guide neurotypical thought (Best et al., 2015; Pellicano & Burr, 2012; Sinha et al., 2014; Leekam et al., 2007).

This divergent approach to cognition, while sometimes challenging in structured environments, is a powerful tool that allows autistic individuals to navigate complexity in unique and effective ways. It highlights the cognitive adaptability and creative problem-solving skills that are often undervalued yet crucial strengths of the autistic mind.

Computational Psychiatry

How can we integrate insights from computational theory in the management and treatment of autism? Computational psychiatry is an interdisciplinary field that applies computational models, mathematical theories, and data-driven approaches to understand, diagnose, and treat mental disorders (Adams et al., 2016; Montague et al., 2012; Goldstein et al., 2018). By integrating insights from neuroscience, psychology, and data science, this field aims to develop more precise diagnostic tools, personalized treatment strategies, and predictive models that can improve patient outcomes and advance our understanding of psychiatric conditions. It integrates principles from neuroscience, psychology, psychiatry, computer science, and data science to provide a quantitative and mechanistic understanding of mental health conditions. The main goal of computational psychiatry is to model underlying cognitive, neural, and behavioral processes contributing to psychiatric disorders to understand them. It seeks to improve diagnosis, predict disease progression, identify biomarkers, and personalize treatment strategies by moving beyond traditional symptom-based classifications. Computational psychiatry provides a framework for understanding the distinct cognitive profiles associated with autism. By examining the ways our brains predict, perceive, and interact with the world, researchers can better appreciate the strengths and challenges of the autistic experience.

Understanding predictive coding and its implications for autism is not just about explaining why autistic individuals struggle in certain areas; it is also about recognizing the depth and capability that come from engaging with the world the autistic way. By valuing these differences, we can begin to see autism not as a condition to be fixed, but as a distinct and valuable way of being.

Towards a Neutral and Non-Pathologizing Framework

A preference for computational theories, particularly in the context of the zero-person perspective, is a strategic choice that aligns with modern, inclusive approaches to autism research. It avoids the pitfalls of pathologizing autistic cognition and provides a strong, non-biased platform for understanding and empirically exploring the unique strengths of autistic individuals. This approach makes the zero-person perspective not only scientifically promising but also ethically and socially progressive.

Computational Models as Inclusive Approaches

Computational theories, such as predictive coding and the Free Energy Principle, offer a neutral, mechanistic view of cognition that does not inherently pathologize autistic traits. These models focus on the brain's information processing and prediction mechanisms, describing how differences in these processes can result in distinct cognitive experiences without labeling them as inherently dysfunctional.

Contrast with Pathologizing Theories

While some theories have historically framed autism in negative, deficit-focused terms (Wing, 1996; Baron-Cohen, 2008), emphasizing challenges in social interaction and communication, more recent approaches advocate for a strengths-based perspective. These newer models highlight the unique cognitive styles and abilities of autistic individuals, advocating for a deeper understanding rather than stigmatization (Pellicano & Burr, 2012).

Zero-Person Cognition as a Solution

Computational models align well with the zero-person approach because they emphasize objective, data-driven analyses that minimize neurotypical biases inherent in first-person accounts. Unlike theories that stem from neurotypical-centric viewpoints, computational approaches allow for a reframing of autistic cognition as a variation of information processing rather than a deficit. This alignment highlights the zero-person perspective as a valuable tool in shifting how autism is conceptualized in cognitive neuroscience.

Reducing Stigmatization through Mechanistic Accounts

Computational models provide a language that describes autistic cognition in terms of altered prediction mechanisms, such as reduced reliance on prior beliefs or heightened attention to sensory data. These descriptions do not carry the moral or societal judgments that are often implicit in theories that link cognitive differences to broader social critiques.

Potential for Empirical Exploration

Although direct empirical studies linking computational models to zero-person cognition are currently limited, there is a clear pathway for future research. Theories like predictive coding are already used to explain many observed characteristics of autistic cognition, such as atypical sensory integration, reduced self-referential thought, and distinctive learning patterns. These theories provide a strong foundation upon which zero-person cognition can be further tested and validated empirically.

Selfhood and the Autistic Self

One of the most intriguing aspects of being autistic is how the condition shapes our sense of self. Growing up, I often felt disconnected—not just from people, but from my own identity. I struggled to understand who I was, how I fit in, and what it meant to have a sense of "self" in the first place. My parents would oftentimes call on me to be more self-assured. For a long time, I thought this was yet another way I was flawed. But as I delve deeper into the science of autism today, I begin to realize that my experience was not a mistake—it was simply different (Nilsson, 2020).[4] This chapter explores how autistic selfhood works, how it diverges from the neurotypical experience, and what that means for those of us living with autism.

The Capacity for Selfhood

Selfhood is often regarded as a hallmark of being human. Selfhood is a continuous thread of identity that weaves together thoughts, feelings, and actions, providing a sense of constancy, centeredness, and groundedness. However, for autistic individuals, this thread may feel frayed or even intermittently absent. The experience of selfhood can be more fragmented and less cohesive, often deeply intertwined with immediate sensory and

---

[4] Research contrasts self-disorders in schizophrenia with autism, emphasizing that while autistic self-processing is different, it remains fundamentally intact and valid. This insight reinforces the argument that autistic cognition represents an alternative, not a pathological state.

32

cognitive states. This does not mean that autistic individuals lack a sense of self entirely; rather, the self-experience operates on different terms, dominated by moment-to-moment perceptions and experiences.

In neurotypical brains, selfhood is constructed through networks that integrate past experiences, future goals, and present states into a cohesive sense of 'me.' This construction is heavily influenced by social interactions, emotional feedback, and cultural norms. Autistic brains, however, often approach selfhood differently. Rather than forming a continuous narrative, their sense of self can be more episodic, less anchored by conventional markers of identity, and more closely tied to the immediate, moment-to-moment flow of experience (Lombardo et al., 2010; Lind, 2010; Crane et al., 2010; Grisdale-Kilgour et al., 2014).

Selfhood in Biological Systems

Understanding selfhood from a biological perspective involves examining how human brains—and even the brains of certain animals—construct the experience of being someone. The human brain excels at self-representation, integrating sensory inputs, memories, emotions, and abstract thinking into a cohesive self-model. For neurotypicals, this process feels seamless, intuitive, and transparent; they simply are who they are without second guessing it.

Autistic individuals, however, may struggle with self-recognition (Cygan, 2019) or find it difficult to connect past, present, and future selves into a cohesive narrative (Lind, 2010; Crane et al. 2010). Our sense of self is often less pronounced, more anchored in the present moment, and heavily influenced by actual cognitive states. This perspective may help explain why routines and rituals are so important. Repeating the same actions or maintaining consistent habits helps us build a sense of permanence or groundedness. Rituals provide a sense of identity and stability.

Paradoxically, we often do not attach ourselves to our accomplishments in the same way neurotypicals might. Graduating, landing a good job, or maintaining a fit physique are all commendable, but they are not necessarily things we define ourselves by.

Artificial Intelligence and Cognitive Systems

Interestingly, researchers have drawn conceptual parallels between the functioning of advanced artificial intelligence systems and certain cognitive processes observed in autism spectrum disorder. For instance, Pellicano and Burr (2012) suggest that individuals with autism may rely more heavily on immediate sensory data rather than prior expectations, a trait that is reminiscent of how AI systems process vast amounts of detailed information without inherent biases. Additionally, Frith and Happé (1994) discuss cognitive styles in autism that emphasize focused information processing, akin to the data-driven approaches seen in AI. These parallels offer valuable insights into both human cognition and the development of AI, highlighting the potential for mutual learning between the fields. However, while AI lacks consciousness and a subjective, continuous sense of self, autistic individuals are conscious beings with their own self-awareness, which may differ from neurotypical patterns but is nonetheless rich and multifaceted (Lombardo et al., 2010).

The kind of immediate, context-dependent processing observed in autistic individuals allows for a unique form of self-awareness that is not burdened by the weight of a continuous identity which can feel liberating overall.

The Phenomenal Self and Self-Model Theory

The concept of the phenomenal self—essentially, the felt sense of being someone—is central to understanding how humans experience themselves. According to Thomas Metzingers self-model theory, our brains create a phenomenal self-model (PSM) that integrates sensory, cognitive, and emotional information into a coherent sense of "I". This self-model is an internal representation of who we are. He argues that the self-model forms the basis for conscious experience, influencing how individuals perceive themselves and interact with the world around them (Metzinger, 2003). Variations in the self-model can influence perception and consciousness (Metzinger, 2004). Conversely, autistic individuals may have a weaker or less integrated phenomenal self-model.

In contrast to the PSM, the concept of Minimal Phenomenal Selfhood (MPS) might help explain this difference. According to Thomas Metzinger, Minimal Phenomenal Selfhood refers to the most basic form of self-experience that consists of the immediate, pre-reflective sense of being a subject of experience situated in the here and now. MPS is characterized by a first-person perspective, bodily self-location, and self-identification, but lacks higher cognitive features like complex autobiographical memories, narrative identity, or personal beliefs. It is a minimal, non-conceptual, and embodied form of self-consciousness that serves as the foundational layer of the self, providing the raw experience of being someone without the narrative and social dimensions typically associated with personal identity. Metzinger uses MPS to argue that even this basic sense of self is a construct of the brain, highlighting the illusionary nature of selfhood (Metzinger, 2003).

So, the MPS is the feeling of being an embodied agent in the here and now, without the constant overlay of who you were or who you might become. Shaun Gallagher distinguishes between the minimal self (immediate sense of presence) and the narrative self (extended, story-like identity) (Gallagher, 2005). This perspective helps frame the autistic experience as uniquely attuned to the present moment rather than bound by an ongoing self-narrative (Milton, 2017), challenging the traditional view of self-deficits in autism.

Studies also show that autistic individuals may not exhibit the same ownership effect seen in neurotypical people, suggesting a distinct approach to self-referential memory. This difference emphasizes a unique relationship between self and memory in autism, further validating the minimal self as a coherent, alternative form of self-awareness (Grisdale et al., 2014).

The Default Mode Network (DMN) and Selfhood

A key player in constructing the self-model is the Default Mode Network (DMN)—a network of brain regions that activates during self-referential thinking, introspection, and daydreaming. The DMN is like the brain's autopilot for self-awareness, continuously running in the background to maintain our sense of who we are.

In autistic individuals, however, the DMN functions differently. Studies have shown that autistic brains exhibit atypical patterns of connectivity within the DMN, which can affect how we experience selfhood. Assaf et al. (2010) found that autistic brains show abnormal functional connectivity within the DMN, particularly between key regions such as the medial prefrontal cortex and posterior cingulate cortex. This altered connectivity is linked to differences in self-referential processing and social cognition, highlighting distinct neural mechanisms underlying self-awareness in autism. Such differences often manifest as increased connectivity within the network, particularly between the posterior cingulate cortex (PCC) and medial prefrontal cortex (mPFC), and reduced connectivity between the DMN and other brain networks (Wang et al., 2021). This altered connectivity might explain why autistic self-awareness feels less seamless and more episodic, fluctuating based on sensory and cognitive inputs rather than a stable internal narrative. Lombardo et al. (2010) concluded that individuals with ASD exhibit decreased activity in anterior and posterior midline regions of the default-mode network during self-specific tasks, leading to difficulties in self-referential processing.

The Epistemic Agent Model and Metacognition

The Epistemic Agent Model (EAM) offers another lens to understand autistic selfhood, focusing more on how we manage knowledge and decision-making. The Epistemic Agent Model, proposed by Thomas Metzinger, refers to a theoretical framework in which an agent is defined by its capacity to acquire, store, and manipulate knowledge about itself and the world. The EAM emphasizes that the agent's self-model is crucial for generating predictions, making decisions, and adapting to the environment. This model integrates an agent's cognitive functions, such as attention, memory, and consciousness, providing insights into how knowledge shapes self-awareness and action (Metzinger, 2017).

So, the EAM emphasizes the agent's ability to understand and control its own knowledge, which is a core aspect of metacognition. Metacognition involves awareness and regulation of one's cognitive processes, such as thinking about thinking, which aligns with EAM's focus on self-monitoring and self-evaluation in decision-making. The EAM thus provides a framework for how metacognitive processes contribute to the sense of self and agency. Metacognition—thinking about our own thinking—is a crucial part of how we regulate our actions and beliefs. But in autism, metacognitive processes can be altered, leading to a self-model that is less reflective and more driven by immediate sensory evidence (Williams, 2010). Williams discusses that individuals with autism often exhibit a specific deficit in self-awareness, particularly in recognizing their own mental states, which can be linked to altered metacognitive processes. The study highlights that while autistic individuals may show typical awareness of the "physical self," their awareness of the "psychological self," which includes reflective thinking and metacognition, is often impaired. This leads to a self-model that relies more on direct, sensory experiences rather than reflective or metacognitive processing.

Metzinger's views on agency underscore that conscious experience of self-control does not necessarily require a stable self-model. For autistic individuals, this suggests that the immediate, sensory-driven experience of agency can be deeply rooted in moment-to-moment interactions, supporting the zero-person perspective (Metzinger, 2013).

Bodily, Attentional, and Cognitive Agency

Agency and the sense of self are deeply interconnected, with agency playing a crucial role in the development and maintenance of one's sense of self. Agency refers to the capacity to initiate, control, and take responsibility for one's actions, thoughts, and decisions. It involves the perception that one's actions influence the environment and that one is the author of those actions. This sense of control and intentionality is fundamental to how we experience ourselves as distinct, autonomous beings. Without a sense of agency, the coherence and stability of the self (model) would be significantly compromised, affecting how one navigates and interprets personal experiences. The following six aspects shed light on how agency and the sense of self are related:

1. **Formation of Self-Identity:** Agency contributes to the formation of self-identity by reinforcing the understanding that one is a separate, autonomous individual capable of influencing the world. Through experiences of making choices and observing the outcomes, individuals build a narrative of who they are based on their actions and intentions.

2. **Self-Attribution and Ownership:** The sense of agency involves the recognition that one's actions are self-generated rather than externally imposed. This self-attribution fosters a sense of ownership over one's thoughts and behaviors, strengthening the boundaries of the self and differentiating it from the external world.

3. **Continuity of Self:** Agency provides a sense of continuity, helping to integrate past actions and intentions into a coherent self-concept. By linking our past, present, and future actions, agency supports the idea of a stable self that persists over time, despite changes in experiences and circumstances.

4. **Emotional Connection and Self-Esteem:** A strong sense of agency is often linked to positive emotions, self-esteem, and confidence. When individuals feel capable of influencing their surroundings and achieving goals, they tend to have a more robust and positive sense of self. Conversely, a diminished sense of agency can lead to feelings of helplessness, disconnection, and a weakened sense of self.

5. **Self-Regulation and Autonomy:** Agency allows individuals to self-regulate their behavior in alignment with personal values, beliefs, and goals. This capacity to act in accordance with one's inner motives rather than external pressures reinforces the sense of being true to oneself, thereby enhancing self-authenticity and integrity.

6. **Perception of Free Will:** The experience of making choices freely, without feeling coerced, is integral to our sense of self. It fosters the perception of being an autonomous agent capable of shaping one's own life, thus contributing to a deeper sense of personal identity and purpose.

Autistic selfhood involves a distinct experience of agency—the sense of control over our bodies, attention, and cognition. For many of us, bodily agency can feel more fragmented, with heightened awareness of physical sensations or challenges in motor coordination. Uddin and Menon (2010) discuss how resting-state fMRI has revealed altered functional connectivity in autistic individuals, particularly noting disruptions in sensorimotor and large-scale brain networks. Additionally, studies by Hamilton et al. (2011) and Lind (2010) highlight how these neural differences contribute to a more fragmented and episodic sense of self, as well as increased sensory sensitivities and motor coordination challenges. Such disruptions are significant because they impact various cognitive and social functions associated with autism, highlighting atypical brain network organization as a characteristic of the condition. A heightened bodily focus can make us hyper-aware of our own movements and internal states, sometimes to the point of distraction.

Attentional agency—the ability to control where we focus—is another area where autistic individuals often differ. Keehn et al. (2013) discuss how individuals with autism often display atypical attentional patterns, including intense, hyper-focused attention on specific details, which can interfere with the ability to shift focus to other tasks or stimuli. This hyper-focus is linked to differences in the functioning of attentional networks in the brain, particularly impairments in disengaging attention, which contribute to the distinctive cognitive and perceptual experiences characteristic of autism. This can be a strength in tasks that require precision but a challenge when flexibility and adaptability are called for (Dajani & Uddin, 2015). Additionally, Oberman and Ramachandran (2007) highlight how these attentional differences may impact social cognition, while Happé and Frith (2020) emphasize the practical implications of hyper-focus in educational and occupational settings. Cognitive agency, which involves higher-level decision-making and planning, can also differ. Autistic individuals may find it harder to switch between tasks or adjust strategies, relying instead on familiar routines and established patterns.

To better grasp the differences between neurotypical and autistic agency, I created a flow chart, visualizing the various aspects and sub aspects of agency. This allows you to identify the aspects that are present, variable or compromised. The classification used in the flow chart aligns with established theories of agency from cognitive science, neuroscience, and psychology. This classification is based on work by Gallagher (2000), Frith et al (2000) and Bandura (1989). Each subcomponent reflects recognized processes that contribute to an individual's overall sense of agency. The following is a summary of the meaning of each aspect in this classification:

1. Bodily Agency
   - **Motor Control**: Motor control is essential in bodily agency, reflecting the ability to execute movement. Research in neuroscience highlights how motor control is closely tied to the brain's sensorimotor systems, contributing significantly to our sense of agency over bodily actions.
   - **Intentionality**: Intentionality refers to the directedness of mental states toward actions and is a crucial component of agency, often studied in the context of cognitive psychology and philosophy.
   - **Sense of Ownership**: The sense of ownership relates to the feeling that one's body or actions belong to oneself,

supported by evidence from neuropsychology and cognitive neuroscience.

- **Proprioception**: Proprioception, or the body's sense of position and movement, plays a crucial role in bodily agency, with studies confirming its influence on how we perceive and control our bodies.

2. Attentional Agency

- **Selective Attention**: Selective attention is the process of focusing on specific stimuli while ignoring others, crucial for goal-directed behavior. This aspect is widely studied in cognitive psychology and neuroscience.
- **Sustained Attention**: This refers to maintaining focus over time, essential for tasks that require prolonged effort. The concept is well-supported in the literature on attentional control and vigilance.
- **Shifting Attention**: Shifting attention, or cognitive flexibility, involves moving focus between tasks or stimuli, supported by research on executive function and cognitive control.
- **Divided Attention**: Divided attention involves managing multiple tasks simultaneously, a well-researched area within cognitive psychology that demonstrates the limits and capacities of human attention.

3. Cognitive Agency

- **Self-Regulation**: Self-regulation is the ability to control one's emotions, thoughts, and behaviors, playing a significant role in cognitive agency. It is extensively studied within psychology, particularly in self-control and goal achievement research.

- **Metacognition**: Metacognition involves awareness and understanding of one's own thought processes. This concept is widely supported in educational psychology and cognitive science as critical to learning and decision-making.
- **Goal Setting**: Goal setting involves defining and pursuing objectives, an essential part of cognitive agency, supported by extensive research in motivation and organizational psychology.
- **Strategic Planning**: Strategic planning refers to setting goals and determining the necessary steps to achieve them, essential in cognitive agency literature, particularly within decision-making research.
- **Adaptability**: Adaptability refers to the ability to adjust to new conditions, a critical component of cognitive agency, supported by evidence in psychological and organizational studies.

If you compare the following three charts, you might get a more intuitive understanding on how agency differs in the autistic experience compared to the normal neurotypical experience. The first chart shows a neurotypical system, the second chart shows a standard interpretation of the autistic experience and the third reflects my evaluation of myself, which can be best described as high functioning autism.

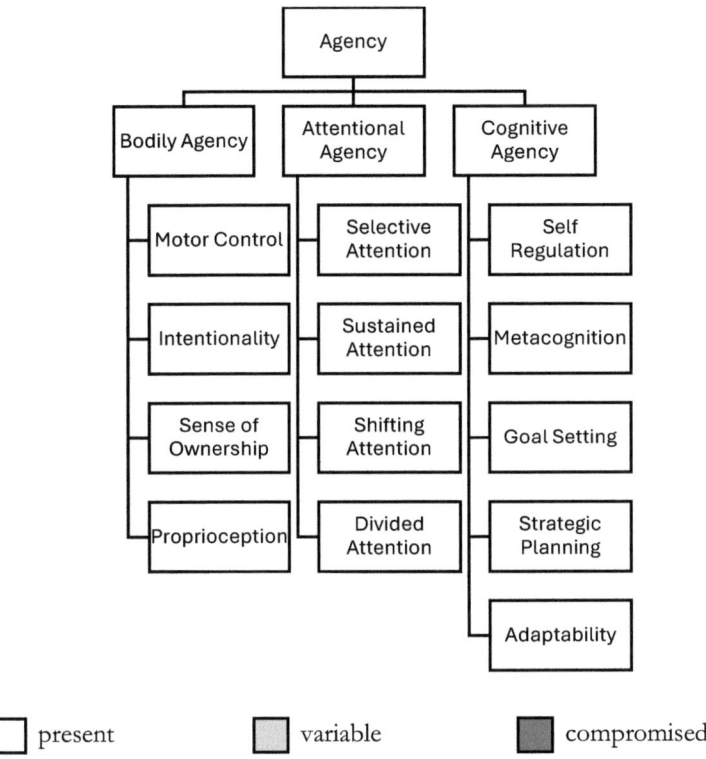

Figure 2 Agency in neurotypical individuals

45

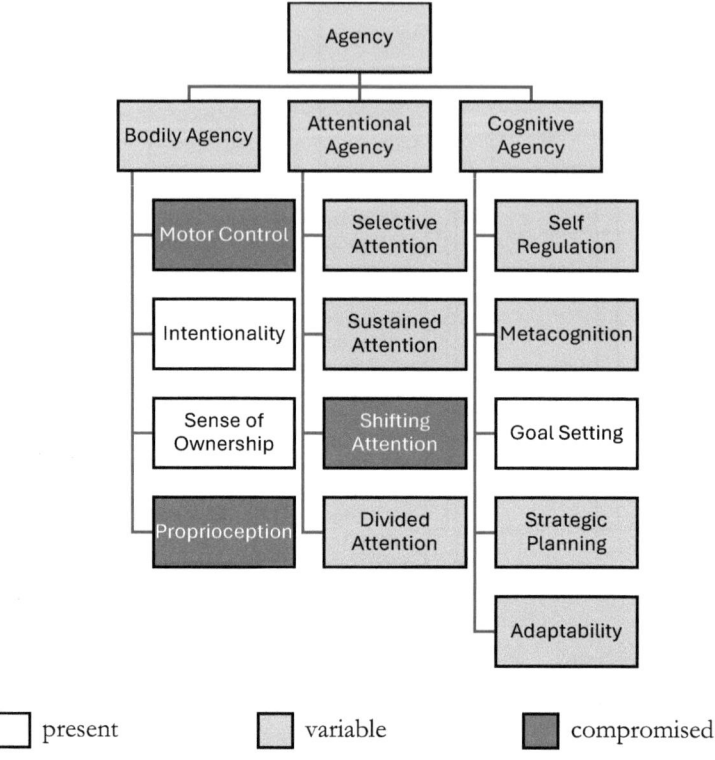

Figure 3 Agency in autistic individuals

The sense of agency and self-ownership in autism often does not align in conventional ways, leading to a more situational and immediate form of self-awareness. This contributes to a sense of self that is context-dependent rather than narratively continuous.

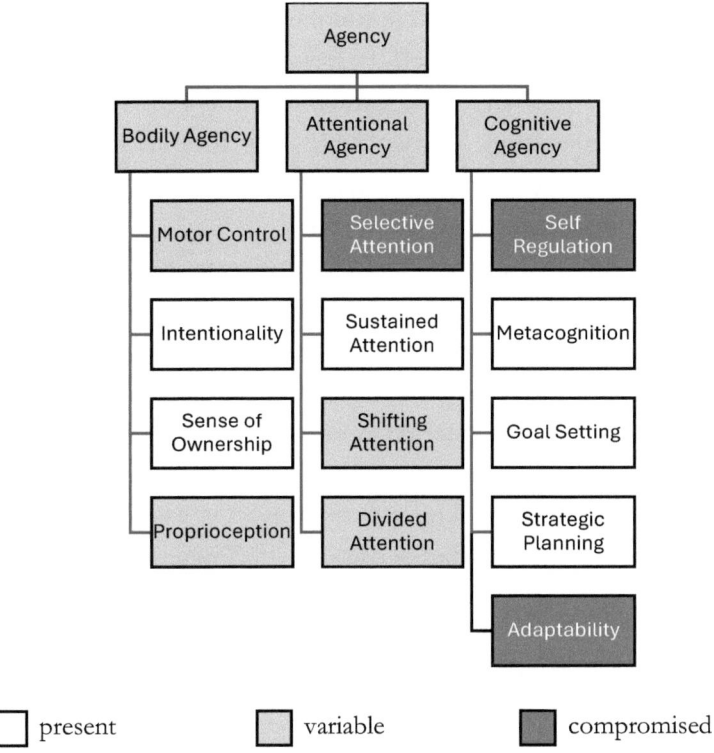

Figure 4 Agency in a high functioning autistic individual

Transparency of the Autistic PSM

Among other factors, the degree of metacognitive ability discussed earlier significantly influences how opaque or transparent the Phenomenal Self Model (PSM) is to any individual. In Metzinger's theory, a transparent PSM means that the self-model is experienced as reality without awareness of its construction, whereas an opaque PSM allows the individual to recognize the model as a construct. High metacognitive abilities enable individuals to reflect on their mental states, making the PSM opaquer. This increased self-awareness allows individuals to recognize the constructed nature of their self-experience, potentially enhancing introspective depth and critical self-reflection, although it may also pose challenges to achieving a coherent and integrated sense of self.

In the context of autism, research suggests that autistic individuals often experience an opaquer phenomenal self-model compared to neurotypical individuals. This means that autistic people are more aware of their self-representational processes, which can lead to a heightened awareness of their thoughts, feelings, and bodily sensations as constructed rather than seamlessly integrated experiences. This phenomenon is associated with a more fragmented, less fluid sense of self. There are several reasons for this:

1. **Heightened Self-Consciousness and Metacognition**: Autistic individuals often report heightened self-awareness and introspection. This increased self-monitoring can contribute to the experience of the self as an object of observation rather than an effortless background process, thus making the self-model more opaque (Lombardo & Baron-Cohen, 2010; Williams, 2010).

2. **Difficulty in Integrating Multisensory Information**: Studies indicate that autistic individuals have challenges integrating multisensory input, which can affect the seamless construction of the self. For example, difficulties in connecting emotional experiences with bodily sensations can lead to a sense of disconnection or awareness of the process,

contributing to an opaque self-experience (Noel et al., 2018; Kew & McIlvane, 2009).

3. **Altered Agency and Self-Other Distinction**: Autistic individuals often experience challenges in distinguishing between self and other, which can lead to a fragmented sense of agency. This struggle can make the self-model feel less automatic and more constructed, thereby increasing opacity (Trevarthen & Delafield-Butt, 2013; Wheelwright et al., 2006).

4. **Cognitive Processing Differences**: Autistic individuals frequently exhibit atypical cognitive processing, such as a preference for detail-focused, analytical thinking. This cognitive style can lead to a more explicit awareness of the processes underlying self-experience (Williams, 2010; Happé & Frith, 2006).

Oftentimes, this circumstance leaves autistic individuals to feel heightened self-consciousness, anxiety, and a sense of being different or misunderstood. Our inner dialogue fluctuates greatly depending on whether we are in a social context or alone. Social situations often trigger a heightened state of self-awareness and anxiety, characterized by self-criticism and confusion about social norms. In contrast, when we are alone, the dialogue often becomes more reflective, comfortable, and aligned with our natural thought processes and interests, providing a sense of relief from the social demands that can feel overwhelming. To make this more tangible for the reader, here are some examples of inner dialogues in both types of situations:

Examples of Inner Dialogue in Social Situations:

1. Anxiety-Focused Dialogue:
   - "Am I talking too much? I don't know when to stop."
   - "Did I say something wrong? They look confused."
   - "Why is everyone laughing? I missed the joke again."

2. Self-Critical or Doubtful Dialogue:
   - "Why can't I just act normal? Everyone else seems to know what to do."
   - "I feel so out of place. They must think I'm weird."
   - "I shouldn't have come. I don't know how to talk to them."

3. Reflective or Analytical Dialogue:
   - "Okay, they smiled. Does that mean they agree, or are they just being polite?"
   - "I don't understand this conversation; maybe it's just me missing something again."
   - "Why do these interactions feel so hard? What am I doing wrong?"

Inner Dialogue When Alone:

When alone, the inner dialogue of an autistic person often shifts significantly, usually toward less anxious and more intro-spective, reflective, or even comforting thoughts. This differ-ence is because the pressure of social interaction is removed, al-lowing them to engage with their thoughts and interests more freely.

1. Calm and Reflective Dialogue:
   o "Finally, I can relax and not worry about what to say."
   o "I'm glad to have time for myself; I understand myself better than anyone else."
   o "I can think things through without rushing or feeling judged."

2. Interest-Focused or Passionate Dialogue:
   o "I can focus on my project now; it makes sense when I can take my time."
   o "I love reading about this topic. I can spend hours just exploring it."
   o "This makes sense. I wish I could talk about this without people getting bored."

3. Self-Comforting or Reassuring Dialogue:
   o "It's okay that I don't fit in there; I fit in here."
   o "I'm doing my best. Social stuff is hard, but it doesn't mean I'm less."
   o "I have my own way of seeing things, and that's okay."

Scale-Free Cognition and the Boundaries of Self

For autistic individuals, the line between the self and the world often feels less defined, allowing us to engage with our environment in ways that are both unique and complex. This chapter delves into the concept of scale-free cognition—a way of thinking about cognition that transcends traditional self-boundaries.

The concept of scale-free cognition as proposed by Levin (2019) provides a novel framework for understanding how cognitive boundaries are determined by the extent of a system's ability to perceive, model, and influence its environment. Levin's theory suggests that cognition is not limited to specific biological structures but can extend across different scales of organization, from individual cells to complex multicellular systems. He proposes the concept of a "cognitive light cone," where the boundaries of cognition expand, or contract based on the organism's capacity for measurement and prediction. To understand scale-free cognition, it helps to picture the mind not as a static entity but as something dynamic and flexible. Imagine such a cognitive light cone, a term borrowed from physics that describes how far information can travel within a system. In the context of the mind, this light cone represents the reach of our cognitive processes—the extent to which our thoughts, perceptions, and actions can engage with the world. For neurotypical people, this cognitive boundary is constrained by the idea of a self. Neurotypical brains prioritize self-relevant information, creating a mental filter that shapes what they notice and how they respond. But in autistic individuals, this filter often works differently. Our cognitive light cone is broader, allowing us to engage with more of the sensory data around us. We do not just see what is relevant to the self; we see a wider array of details, patterns, and nuances that might otherwise go unnoticed.

Studies indicate that autistic individuals may have an increased perceptual capacity, allowing them to process more sensory details than neurotypicals, which can lead to an enhanced awareness of environmental nuances that others might filter out as irrelevant. Mottron et al. (2006) found that individuals with autism often have increased perceptual capacity, which means they can process more sensory input simultaneously compared to neurotypical individuals. A more recent study by Tullo et al. (2023) corroborates these findings, further highlighting the enhanced detail-focused processing characteristic of autism spectrum disorders. The study found that autistic individuals often exhibit increased perceptual capacity compared to neurotypicals, allowing them to process more information at any given time.

This increased perceptual capacity in autism can make it harder for autistic individuals to ignore distractions and maintain focus on task-relevant stimuli. Such sensory differences can lead to a less distinct boundary between self-relevant and external information, making it challenging for autistic individuals to prioritize self-focused data over the wider sensory environment (Mottron et al., 2006; Plaisted et al., 2001; Schiltz et al., 2013; Lombardo et al., 2010).

An expanded cognitive boundary can be both a gift and a challenge. It means we are often more attuned to the world, picking up on subtle changes but it also means that the usual buffers that protect the self from overwhelming sensory input are less effective.

The distinct self-model in autism has broader implications for how we understand cognition. By engaging with the world from a more immediate, less self-referential perspective, autistic individuals can access a form of cognition that feels less bound by conventional constraints. This scale-free approach to thinking allows us to engage directly with our environment, often bypassing the usual filters that shape neurotypical perception.

The Role of Bioelectricity and Boundary Modulation

A fascinating aspect of how our cognitive boundaries are formed involves bioelectricity—the electric signals that govern how cells communicate and organize themselves. Recent research suggests that these signals play a crucial role in shaping not just our bodies but our minds, influencing how we perceive and engage with the world. Michael Levin and colleagues have extensively explored how bioelectricity acts as a foundational component in the development of cognition, suggesting that bioelectric networks could serve as a "cognitive glue" that enables the scaling of basic cellular functions into complex behaviors and cognitive states. Their work shows that these electrical signals contribute to the formation of not just the physical body but also cognitive frameworks, highlighting a deep connection between physiology and cognition across different scales of life, from simple organisms to humans (Levin, 2022). Moreover, this research has demonstrated that bioelectric signals influence how cells establish patterns that guide brain development, suggesting that these signals might contribute to the organization of neural circuits responsible for perception and decision-making. This work emphasizes the potential of bioelectricity as a key factor in shaping how organisms, including humans, perceive and interact with their environment, bridging the gap between cellular-level organization and higher cognitive functions.

While direct evidence linking bioelectric variations to cognitive differences in autism is still developing, it is reasonable to assume that atypical bioelectric signaling could influence neural connectivity and sensory processing, which are commonly altered in autism.

Decentralization and Robustness

One of the core strengths of scale-free cognition is its decentralized nature. Unlike neurotypical thinking, which often centers on a self-focused perspective, scale-free cognition operates without a clear hierarchy. This decentralization makes it more robust, adaptable, and resilient to change. In autistic cognition, this means that our thinking is not confined by the usual top-down processes that prioritize self-relevance. Instead, our minds are free to explore a broader range of information, drawing connections that might seem unconventional or unexpected. Scale-free cognition, characterized by its decentralized nature, suggests a form of thinking that does not adhere to strict hierarchical structures. This makes it more adaptable and resilient, allowing for a broader, more flexible engagement with information.

Efficiency and Emergence

One more aspect of scale-free cognition is how it allows for efficiency through emergence—where complex behaviors arise from simple rules. In the context of autism, this means that our thinking often operates on principles that are highly adaptable, allowing us to respond to situations with a kind of intuitive logic that does not rely on prior expectations.

Reduction of Cognitive Biases

Another advantage of scale-free cognition is its potential to reduce cognitive biases. Because autistic thinking often operates outside of the usual self-centered frameworks, we are less likely to fall into common traps like confirmation bias or emotional reasoning. Our focus on immediate sensory data means we engage with information more directly, without the filters that can distort perception. This objectivity can be incredibly powerful, allowing autistic individuals to approach problems with a level of clarity that is less influenced by personal preconceptions.

Counterarguments: Lack of Subjective Understanding and Introspection

Of course, scale-free cognition is not without its challenges. One of the trade-offs is a reduced capacity for subjective understanding and introspection. Because autistic thinking often prioritizes external data over internal reflection, we might struggle with tasks that require deep self-awareness or emotional insight. For me, this means that while I am highly attuned to the world around me, my internal landscape can feel less accessible, less defined. A good example is a classical talk therapy session where the therapist typically opens the session with the question: "So, how are you feeling today?" For an autistic person there is no obvious answer. It is more like we must go look for it. We must first inquire how we are feeling and then try and translate this into words. If we took the time we needed, the hour would likely be up by the time we came up with an answer. This is not a flaw, but a different way of being. It is a reminder that all cognitive styles come with their own strengths and weaknesses. The key is to understand and appreciate these differences, recognizing the value in each unique way of engaging with the world.

The idea of scale-free cognition opens new avenues for understanding autistic thinking. It suggests that our cognitive boundaries are more flexible, more adaptable, and less constrained by the usual limits of selfhood. This perspective not only helps explain the strengths of autistic cognition but also challenges traditional views of what it means to think, perceive, and be.

Conditions for the Zero-Person Perspective

Living with an autistic mind often means navigating a world in which you do not seem to fit. The way we think, process, and engage with our surroundings is different from the norm, and understanding as well as navigating these differences will be a lifelong effort.

The idea of a zero-person perspective might sound counterintuitive for neurotypicals, but for autistic individuals, it is a way of life. It is a mode of thinking and perceiving that is not centered on the self, unlike the typical first-person perspective most people operate from. Paradoxically, for us, cognition can feel both more detached and more direct at the same time, as if we are engaging with the world without the usual self-referential filters.

Phillips' (2018) discussion of the "explanatory gap" emphasizes the challenges in understanding subjective experiences, drawing parallels to broader philosophical issues in consciousness. This analogy can be extended to understanding autistic cognition from a neurotypical standpoint, highlighting autistic perceptual experiences as unique but coherent cognitive styles. Such framing aligns with discussions on the nature of subjective experience and the difficulties inherent in fully comprehending it from an external viewpoint (Pellicano & Burr, 2012; Lombardo et al., 2010).

To clarify the differentiation between necessary and sufficient conditions for the emergence of a zero-person perspective, particularly in the context of autistic and neurotypical individuals, it is essential to focus on what conditions are inherent (necessary) and which conditions can be cultivated (sufficient).

Necessary Conditions

Necessary conditions are those that must be present for the zero-person perspective to occur. For autistic individuals, certain neurobiological and cognitive traits naturally predispose them to this perspective. A key necessary condition is the atypical functioning of the Default Mode Network (DMN). Research indicates that in autistic individuals, the DMN is often less active or connected differently, which reduces self-referential thinking and diminishes the focus on social cognition. This neurobiological baseline creates an environment where self-perception and social evaluation are minimized, aligning with broader philosophical discussions about the nature of subjective experience and the challenges of fully understanding it from an outside viewpoint (Uddin et al., 2013; Lombardo et al., 2011; Bennett et al., 2012).

Sufficient Conditions

Sufficient conditions are those that can lead to a zero-person perspective but are not strictly required. Neurotypical individuals, who do not naturally have reduced DMN activity, can achieve a zero-person state through certain practices that mimic these neurocognitive conditions. For example, mindfulness meditation, contemplative practices, and other mental training can reduce DMN activity and enhance non-self-referential processing (Farb et al., 2007; Brewer et al., 2011). These practices do not necessarily change the fundamental structure of the DMN but can alter its functioning temporarily, allowing neurotypical individuals to experience this altered cognitive style.

In autistic cognition, efficient information processing in non-social contexts and the ability to analyze data without personal or emotional interference often arise as a natural part of their cognitive profile (Happé & Frith, 2006). For neurotypical individuals, however, engaging in training that promotes focused attention, objective analysis, and reduction of self-referential thoughts can suffice to induce a 'zero-person perspective'—a cognitive state characterized by minimal self-referential processing and increased present-moment awareness (Farb et al., 2007; Brewer et al., 2011). These practices do not necessarily change the fundamental structure of the Default Mode Network (DMN) but can alter its functioning temporarily, allowing neurotypical individuals to experience this altered cognitive style.

Autistic individuals naturally meet the necessary conditions (altered DMN activity) and often have sufficient conditions (cognitive processing strengths) that align with the zero-person perspective.

Neurotypical Individuals do not naturally meet the necessary conditions but can achieve the sufficient conditions (through practices like meditation) to temporarily adopt a zero-person perspective.

Efficacy of the Zero-Person Perspective in the Human Brain

The zero-person perspective is not just a quirk of autistic cognition; it is a highly efficient way of processing information. Without the added burden of self-reflection, emotional involvement, or social considerations, the brain can allocate more resources to immediate tasks. This efficiency is something I have come to rely on. While others might get bogged down by personal biases or emotional responses, my mind tends to stay on track.

Benefits of Zero-Person Cognition

Scale-free cognition, and by extension the zero-person perspective, can be seen as superior in specific contexts—particularly those requiring adaptability, objectivity, and robust decision-making. Autistic decision-making often defies conventional logic—not because it is irrational, but because it follows a different set of rules. The zero-person perspective plays a crucial role in shaping how we approach decisions, driven by a blend of objective data processing, reduced reliance on emotional cues, and a focus on direct engagement with the world.

Zero-person epistemic agency can be a term that captures the particularities of autistic cognition. Unlike first-person agency, which is deeply personal, and subjective, zero-person agency is more detached and data-driven. For autistic individuals, this means that our cognition often bypasses the filters of personal experience, focusing instead on what the data tells us.

Research consistently shows that autistic individuals excel in tasks that require objective analysis, pattern recognition, and logical reasoning. Our reduced reliance on the DMN plays a key role here, freeing us from the mental loops that often cloud judgment in neurotypical cognition.

High-functioning autistic individuals often demonstrate remarkable efficiencies in information processing, particularly in non-social contexts. This efficiency is directly linked to our unique cognitive architecture.

This processing style is not just about being fast; it is about being precise. It is why so many autistic people excel in fields like mathematics, engineering, and the sciences—areas where objective analysis and attention to detail are paramount.

Ethical, Social, and Cognitive Implications of Zero-Person Decision-Making

Embracing the zero-person perspective is not just about understanding how autistic cognition works; it is about finding ways to live fully within this unique way of being. For autistic individuals, the zero-person perspective can be a path to clarity, precision, and a deeper engagement with the world. But it also comes with its own set of challenges—navigating social expectations, managing sensory sensitivities, and finding balance in a world that often feels out of sync with our ways of thinking.

The zero-person perspective brings with it unique ethical and social implications, especially when it comes to decision-making. On one hand, autistic objectivity can be a powerful asset, allowing us to make unbiased choices that are less influenced by personal or emotional factors. On the other hand, this detachment can also pose challenges, particularly in contexts that require social awareness, societal nuance and emotional consideration.

The ethical implications of the zero-person perspective extend beyond personal decision-making. In many ways, autistic objectivity can lead to more impartial and fair outcomes, especially in situations that benefit from unbiased reasoning. However, this same apparent detachment can also be perceived as a lack of empathy or emotional engagement, particularly in contexts where human-centric values are paramount. Chevallier et al. (2012) argue that autistic individuals often show diminished social motivation, which affects their engagement with social information and can be perceived as a lack of empathy or emotional connection. This detachment can lead to misunderstandings in social interactions, where their unbiased and objective perspective might be misinterpreted as a lack of emotional engagement, especially in contexts that value empathy and personal connection.

Autistic empathy operates differently, often connecting deeply with specific contexts or stimuli rather than following typical social cues. This reframing of empathy challenges traditional views and highlights the validity of alternative social engagement methods (Milton, 2012; Samson, Walker, & Cerniglia, 2014; Gray & Baron-Cohen, 2008).

Differentiating the Zero-Person concept from Meditation, Flow, and Non-Dual States

The term zero-person has been used in various philosophical and meditative contexts to describe states of consciousness where the usual sense of self fades, and awareness becomes detached from personal identity.[5] These states are often sought in meditation, flow, and non-dual awareness practices, reflecting a cognitive mode that contrasts sharply with the self-referential thinking typical of everyday consciousness. However, while the zero-person perspective in these traditions shares some similarities with the cognitive style often seen in autistic individuals, it is crucial to distinguish the concepts to repurpose the term specifically for autism research.

---

[5] A recent study by Katyal & Goldin (2021) suggest that concentrative meditation enables a nonevaluative perceptual stance, supported by reduced gamma-band phase synchrony in lateral-parietal and occipital regions.

This chapter explores the existing usage of the zero-person concept in meditation and flow states, highlighting the key differences and reframing it to capture the unique cognitive experiences of autistic individuals. By doing so, I aim to further specify a definition of zero-person cognition that is firmly rooted in the context of neurodiversity and autism.

Zero-Person vs. No-Self

In meditative traditions, particularly within Buddhism and Advaita Vedanta, the concept of "no-self" (anatta or anatman) plays a central role. Practitioners of meditation strive to transcend their ego-driven identities, experiencing a state of consciousness where personal narrative and self-referential thought dissolve.[6] This state is often described as a zero-person experience—consciousness without a personal center—where the individual perceives the world without the filter of the ego. Berkovich-Ohana et al. (2012) were able to show that mindfulness meditation practitioners exhibit lower frontal gamma activity, mainly right-lateralized, related to self-reference and default mode network (DMN) activity. This trait reduction in frontal gamma power suggests a shift from narrative self-reference to experiential self-reference mode. In a more recent study, Berkovich-Ohana et al. (2024) suggest that meditative practices lead to a reorganization of the self-pattern towards a 'selfless' state.

While the meditative zero-person state is a cultivated experience, often requiring years of practice, the zero-person perspec-

---

[6] A study by Laukkonen & Slagter (2021)suggests that meditation can reduce temporally extended processes like episodic future thinking and decision making, and may lead to unusual experiences such as loss of self-other distinction and cessation of time in non-dual awareness.

tive as seen in autism represents a more natural and continuous cognitive style that does not necessarily involve deliberate effort to minimize the self. This form of cognition can be understood as a baseline mode of processing, rather than an altered state achieved through intentional mental training.

The meditative zero-person state emphasizes transcendence of the self as a spiritual goal, whereas the autistic zero-person perspective is not about seeking transcendence but reflects a fundamental way of being. This difference is critical; the zero-person perspective in autism is not an escape from self but rather a different cognitive style that prioritizes direct interaction with the world without the mediation of self-referential thought. Therefore, while both contexts share a reduction of self-awareness, the zero-person perspective in autism is inherent and situational, rather than aspirational or transcendental.

Flow States vs. Zero-Person Perspective in Autism

Detached awareness, often described in the context of meditation and flow states, involves a sense of being fully present without the usual self-conscious concerns. In these states, the individual experiences a merging of action and awareness, where thoughts and actions flow effortlessly without the interjection of personal judgment or reflective self-awareness.

Flow, a concept extensively studied by Mihaly Csikszentmihalyi (1990), describes a state where individuals are deeply absorbed in an activity, losing track of time and self-consciousness. The focus is on the task itself rather than on personal gain or social judgment. While flow states and the meditative zero-person states align superficially with the zero-person perspective in autism—particularly in the shared reduction of self-referential thought—there are fundamental differences.

The flow state is typically transient and tied to specific activities that align personal skills with challenges. It is characterized by a deliberate engagement in a task that results in a temporary suspension of self-awareness. Conversely, the zero-person perspective in autism is not dependent on external tasks or specific conditions but is instead a stable cognitive trait. Autistic individuals often experience this direct, unfiltered engagement with their environment as a constant way of interacting with the world, rather than an episodic state triggered by circumstances.

Philosophically, the meditative and flow-based zero-person states often serve as idealized or sought-after experiences in contrast to the default neurotypical human condition. In contrast, the zero-person perspective in autism reflects a default mode of processing that can be both advantageous and challenging, depending on the context. It is not a state to be attained but a natural, ongoing way of experiencing reality.

Repurposing Zero-Person for Autism Research

Repurposing the zero-person concept for autism research highlights a crucial point: while the meditative and flow-based uses of the term suggest an exceptional state achieved through deliberate practice, the zero-person perspective in autism represents a distinctive cognitive style that exists independently of such efforts.

This perspective challenges traditional views of selfhood that dominate Western philosophy, which often centers on a stable, continuous self as the essence of personal identity. The zero-person perspective in autism suggests a different model of selfhood—one that is fluid, episodic, and context-dependent. This mode of being does not diminish the richness of experience but reframes it, presenting a way of interacting with the world that is deeply authentic and unmediated.

By distinguishing the zero-person perspective in autism from its philosophical and meditative counterparts, we assert its unique relevance to neurodiversity and autism research. This approach invites a rethinking of how we define cognitive diversity, moving away from a deficit-focused view and toward an appreciation of the distinct ways autistic individuals perceive and engage with reality. Recognizing the zero-person perspective as a legitimate and valuable cognitive style opens new avenues for understanding and supporting neurodivergent minds.

Distinctions Between Zero-Person Cognition and Existing Cognitive Theories

Zero-person cognition serves as a novel framework that reinterprets existing symptoms of autism (e.g., reduced self-referential thought, enhanced attention to detail, and objective reasoning) not as deficits but as equally valid cognitive strengths. This perspective shift reframes autism from a deficit-based model to a value-based model that highlights the strengths and distinctiveness of autistic cognition. Zero-Person Cognition vs. No-Self in Meditation

Unlike the no-self-concept, zero-person cognition is not deliberately cultivated but is a baseline cognitive mode often observed in autistic individuals. It reflects a natural cognitive style where self-referential thought is minimized, and perception is directly rooted in sensory input and immediate experience. The distinction lies in the fact that zero-person cognition is not an achieved state but an inherent way of processing information.

Zero-Person Cognition vs. First-Person and Third-Person Perspectives

The First-Person perspective is centered on the self, with cognition highly influenced by personal experiences, biases, and emotions. It is the default mode for most neurotypical individuals and is characterized by a continuous self-narrative.

The Third-Person perspective involves understanding situations from an outside viewpoint, often associated with objective reasoning and detachment from personal biases.

Distinct from both first-person and third-person perspectives, zero-person cognition does without a self-centered narrative. It focuses on direct interaction with the environment without the overlay of personal identity or social expectations. This perspective shifts the locus of cognition from self-referential thinking to a direct, immediate engagement with the external world, which is particularly relevant in the context of autism.

Zero-Person Cognition vs. Predictive Coding and Bayesian Brain Theories

Predictive Coding and Bayesian Brain Theories describe the brain as a predictive machine that constantly updates its model of the world by minimizing prediction errors. In neurotypicals, this model is heavily shaped by past experiences and social norms, often leading to a bias toward expected outcomes.

While predictive coding also applies to autistic cognition, zero-person cognition emphasizes the autistic brain's reduced reliance on these past experiences and social norms. This leads to a cognitive style that prioritizes real-time sensory data over previously learned expectations, resulting in unique ways of perceiving and interacting with the world that are not merely predictive but are immediate and unfiltered.

Zero-Person Cognition vs. Self-Model Theory

Metzinger's Self-Model theory posits that the self is a constructed model created by the brain to facilitate interaction with the world. It includes elements such as the phenomenal self-model, which integrates sensory, cognitive, and emotional information into a coherent sense of "I."

In contrast, zero-person cognition does not prioritize the construction of a cohesive self-model. It often results in a fragmented or episodic sense of self, where cognitive processing is more fluid and context dependent. The focus is less on maintaining a consistent narrative and more on directly responding to sensory and situational stimuli, which aligns with how many autistic individuals experience their cognition.

Part 2 – Experience

Adopting the Zero Person Concept

In the second part of this book, we move from understanding the scientific foundations of the zero-person perspective to exploring its practical impact on daily life. This chapter serves as a gateway to actively embracing the zero-person perspective, offering tools and insights to incorporate into everyday routines and interactions. There is a caveat: autism is a spectrum, and I can only speak for myself. I will present you with the skills and tools that work for me, knowing full well that everyone else on the spectrum might need to find different solutions for themselves, depending on their individual sensory profile. What I do know is that had I known about the zero-person perspective sooner and had I learned about self-care early on, both two episodes of clinical depression and a burnout could have probably been prevented. So, take from my notes what works for you, leave the rest and start building your own toolkit.

The chapters that follow will guide you through essential skills, from building routines and managing sensory sensitivities to navigating social relationships and advocating for your needs. By adopting the zero-person perspective, you are not just adjusting to a new way of thinking about your autism—you can start redefining how you interact with the world around you in a way that works for you. Rather than adapting to and coping with a neurotypical reality, you can start to define an autistic reality that lessens your challenges and fosters your strengths. This is a journey that emphasizes self-care, empowerment, and the importance of setting boundaries, helping you to become an active participant in creating a more inclusive and understanding environment in which you can thrive.

Throughout this section, you will learn how to leverage the zero-person perspective to build resilience, foster meaningful connections, and advocate for a more neurodiverse-friendly world. As you engage with the strategies and reflections in this chapter, you are encouraged to view challenges as opportunities for growth, positioning yourself not only as a learner but also as an advocate for change. We can only change the world to our favor when we start advocating for ourselves, from our perspective.

Daily Living Skills

Daily living skills are not just about performing tasks; they are about creating a life that works in harmony with one's neurological profile. For autistic individuals, this means embracing strategies that prioritize predictability, self-care, and sensory management. By building supportive routines, engaging in thoughtful self-care practices, and actively managing sensory sensitivities, those on the spectrum can create environments that not only accommodate their needs but also allow them to thrive. These daily practices form the foundation upon which a fulfilling and balanced life can be built, embracing the zero-person perspective to navigate the world with greater autonomy and ease.

Building Routines and Structure

For autistic individuals, routines and structure can serve as vital anchors in everyday life. Science has shown us that our sense of self depends in large parts on how we manage our environment. When your brain is wired such that, it responds to sensory input more than it relies on prior beliefs, a large part of your well-being will come from exerting control over what you can control, to limit surprises. A predictable routine reduces uncertainty, allowing the brain to conserve cognitive resources that would otherwise be expended on navigating unexpected changes. This sense of order is not merely about habit; it is a tool that helps manage sensory sensitivities, reduce anxiety, and foster a sense of groundedness.

Routines can take many forms, from morning rituals like preparing a specific breakfast to meticulously planned schedules for daily tasks. The key is personalization—finding what works best for you. For some, a physical schedule with symbols or colors can provide a clear, tangible roadmap for the day. For others, smartphone apps with reminders and alarms help maintain order.

The ways and means you organize yourself will also greatly depend on your sensory base line. When you just come out of a shutdown or a meltdown[7], you will have to cope with worsened symptoms, and you might need a simpler routine. Prepare for both. Coming back from my last inpatient stay in a psychiatric hospital for the treatment of a clinical depression, I needed a large, physical magnetic board to manage my week. I thought of

---

[7] Shutdown: A shutdown is an internalized response to overwhelm. During a shutdown, an autistic person may withdraw, become non-responsive, or appear to "zone out." This response is characterized by a reduction in interaction with the environment and others, and the person may find it difficult to speak, move, or process what is happening around them. Meltdown: A meltdown is an externalized response to overwhelming situations. It is often characterized by an intense and uncontrollable expression of emotions, which can include crying, shouting, aggressive behavior, or other forms of physical expression. Meltdowns occur when an individual's capacity to cope with overwhelming sensory, emotional, or social input is exceeded, leading to a loss of self-control.

the different activities I would need to engage in, such as working, cooking, walking the dog, housekeeping, and things I would want to engage in such as taking a nap, meditating or painting. For each category I prepared several magnetic strips, each category with a different color. In the beginning I needed to plan out the whole week. I put the board up in my living room, so I would pass by it numerous times a day. Each time I would look at it, I was assured that my week was planned out, I knew exactly what to do next, and I stuck to the plan. With time, I was able to move some things around or rather than planning the whole week ahead of time, I would use the board to keep tabs of what I had done on that day. At the end of a day, I took a marker and drew a smiley face if the day had worked well, a neutral one if it had been ok and a sad face if it had not gone well at all. Keeping tabs like that made me realize how much cognitive load my system would be able to handle at any given time, what helped me and what I needed to avoid. After a couple of months, I did not need the board anymore, but for those first three months or so it was a life saver.

Establishing routines does not have to be rigid or overwhelming. Start with small, manageable steps, such as setting a consistent time for meals or creating a bedtime ritual. Over time, these routines can expand, providing a comforting framework that helps you navigate your day with greater ease. Moreover, incorporating flexibility within these routines—like planning time for unstructured activities—can help prepare for and manage the inevitable disruptions that life brings.

Enhancing predictability also includes keeping tabs on chores and social contact. Both are likely to take tolls on your nervous system, depending on your sensitivities. I had to learn the hard way that talking on the phone for an hour required me to plan for a nap afterwards, just to keep my nervous system in check. A good rule of thumb is to only call someone or only answer a call if you feel your energy reserves are full. It is a very good idea to let your friends and family know ahead of time that you will have to prioritize your energy management over being reachable. Make it known that you require alone time to self-regulate and stay healthy.

A couple of years in since my diagnosis, I no longer require rigorous planning, but I have kept a couple of fixed points in my day that I stick to. I have found that if I let go of those, my balance is jeopardized right away.

The Importance of Self-Care

Self-care is essential for everyone, but for autistic individuals, it often requires more effort and more planning. Self-care encompasses a range of activities designed to maintain physical, mental, and emotional health, from basic hygiene practices to more nuanced needs like sensory management and mental health support. For many on the autism spectrum, engaging in self-care can be challenging due to heightened sensory sensitivities or executive functioning difficulties. We tend to focus too much on tasks and forget our own wellbeing in the process.

Incorporating regular breaks throughout the day to decompress and engage in self-regulating activities, such as meditating, or spending time in nature, can be incredibly beneficial. I have a dog, so I must go for walks several times a day. My dog is my best friend, but he also serves a purpose. He serves as my anchor of sorts. It is almost like he keeps me grounded. There were times when he literally saved me. He would recognize when I would verge on a panic attack, slow his pace and walk me home. So, we take turns walking each other.

It is also crucial to establish a self-care routine that includes exercise, balanced nutrition, and adequate sleep. These foundational aspects of health are often disrupted in autistic individuals due to sensory challenges, making it even more important to approach them with tailored strategies. I have found that weight-lifting helps me feel in my body more. I never had much of a relationship with my body and depending on my state of mind, it would feel in the way. Once something works, autistic individuals tend to stick to it and incorporate it into their routine. This can result in having the same meal for a couple of days in a row, which probably is not the healthiest way to be. We tend to slip into unhealthy routines more easily too, so self-care with regards to bodily needs require consideration. The better you are organized the less you must think about mundane things. If you like to eat a particular dish, think of two more you like equally and rotate between those three to avoid malnourishment.

Mental self-care, such as setting boundaries, engaging in hobbies, or simply allowing time to relax, should be thought of as well. Cognitive overload is common in autism, so regularly assessing one's mental state and knowing when to step back or how to seek support is key. For me, I easily get tinnitus when my nervous system goes into overload. It is like a built-in early warning system. I have learned to take those signs seriously and to react accordingly. Example: I have been writing on this book all day today. Now I realize I have tinnitus, so I will put down the computer and return to writing in a couple of days.

Managing Sensory Sensitivities

Sensory sensitivities are a hallmark of autistic experience, often making everyday environments overwhelming. Managing these sensitivities is not just about avoiding uncomfortable stimuli but actively creating sensory-safe spaces that promote comfort and functionality. This might include adjusting lighting, reducing noise levels, or choosing clothing that is soft and non-restrictive.

One of the first steps in managing sensory sensitivities is to conduct a personal sensory audit—identifying specific triggers and the times of day or environments where they are most prevalent. From there, implementing sensory tools like fidget devices, sunglasses, or custom earphones can provide immediate relief in challenging situations.

Creating a sensory toolkit is another effective strategy. This toolkit might include items such as calming scents, textured fabrics, or small objects that can be manipulated discreetly. These tools can be carried daily and used whenever sensory overload threatens to disrupt functioning. For example, carrying a pair of ear defenders can help manage noisy environments, while a small, scented oil might provide comfort in overwhelming situations.

Let me give you an example for sensory sensitivities. As I am sitting here, writing this book, there is an airplane flying overhead, and some neighbor's oven is giving off a beeping sound. Even though both sounds are far away, they are equally loud to me, and they are massively distracting. What started out a calm Sunday morning is now turning into the bustling concoction of western civilization starting a new day. I will have to put on my noise cancellation headphones if I am to continue writing.

For me, noise-canceling headphones are a must have. I wear them for about half the time I am awake and most times when I am outside. I equally rely on sunglasses and on wearing a beanie a lot. All these accessories serve a purpose. Apart from the apparent purposes, they all give me comfort and a sense of protection. Without them, I feel vulnerable, like a raw egg without a shell.

It is also essential to design a sensory-friendly living space. Home should be a sanctuary—an environment that supports relaxation and recovery. This might mean organizing clutter to reduce visual distractions, using blackout curtains to block out harsh light, or setting up a quiet corner with soft textures and soothing colors. These adjustments, though small, can significantly impact sensory regulation and overall quality of life. I personally prefer natural lighting conditions to artificial lighting, so I hardly turn on my lights, even in winter, except for when I need to perform a task like cooking or reading.

Social Skills and Relationships

Navigating social situations with preparation, building friendships through shared interests, and respecting boundaries and consent all contribute to healthier, more rewarding social connections. By embracing unique communication styles and cultivating environments that feel safe and supportive, autistic individuals can forge meaningful relationships that honor their perspective. The goal is not to conform to neurotypical social norms but to redefine what social success looks like through the lens of the zero-person perspective—focusing on genuine connections that are more purpose than ego driven.

Navigating Social Situations

Social interactions can be particularly challenging for autistic individuals, often due to difficulties in reading social cues, understanding unspoken rules, and having to manage sensory sensitivities at the same time. Embracing the zero-person perspective in social situations paradoxically translates into knowing exactly who you are and what you need to be able to engage meaningfully.

One effective approach is to prepare for social interactions in advance. This could involve familiarizing oneself with the setting, planning conversation topics, or mentally rehearsing potential social scenarios. To neurotypicals this might sound exaggerated. However, adopting the zero-person perspective means acknowledging our deficits and developing tools that help us bridge gaps. We should not have to live isolated lives, just because certain skills do not come naturally to us.

Understanding and setting boundaries is another critical aspect of navigating social situations. Autistic individuals may feel pressured to conform to social expectations that are uncomfortable or overwhelming to them. They default to masking[8]. Masking can involve a range of strategies, such as mimicking facial expressions, tone of voice, or body language of neurotypical people; suppressing autistic behaviors like stimming (repetitive movements or sounds); and forcing oneself to make eye contact. While masking can help autistic people fit in, it often comes at a significant emotional and psychological cost. It can lead to exhaustion, anxiety, depression, and a sense

---

[8] Masking refers to the practice of camouflaging or hiding one's autistic traits to fit in. This behavior is commonly adopted by autistic individuals to avoid being judged, misunderstood, or ostracized.

of inauthenticity, as the individual is constantly working to hide their true self (Hull et al., 2017). Masking is particularly prevalent among autistic women and girls, who are often underdiagnosed compared to males. They may be more likely to mask due to social pressures to conform to gender expectations (Lai et al., 2017).

Learning to politely decline invitations when anxious or to excuse oneself when feeling overstimulated can help maintain a sense of balance. For example, having a set phrase ready, such as "I need to step outside for a moment," can provide a quick exit strategy when social situations become too intense.

Another key aspect of navigating social environments is identifying safe and supportive people. Connecting with individuals who respect your communication style and are aware of your needs can create a more positive social experience. It is also helpful to identify and communicate personal needs clearly; for example, letting friends know about sensory sensitivities or preferences for quieter settings can greatly improve social interactions. I have joined a dinner party wearing my headphones to block out ambient noise and be able to join the conversation. My friends were understanding, and the evening was a good experience for everyone attending, including myself. The more we talk about sensory sensitivities and create awareness for our cognitive differences, the greater our chances are that neurotypicals will meet us halfway.

Building and Maintaining Friendships

Building friendships is a deeply rewarding but often burdensome task for autistic individuals. Unlike the neurotypical emphasis on spontaneous and unstructured socializing, autistic individuals may benefit from more structured approaches to making and maintaining connections. Shared interests, predictable routines, and clear communication can form the basis of meaningful and lasting friendships. Looking back to my childhood and adolescence years, I had one good friend. We lived in the same apartment building and were as close as sisters. At the time, I did not know I was autistic, but I would often insist staying home or engaging in familiar activities. To my friend that must have been rather boring, but we managed to compromise a lot. The word compromise was a fixture in our vocabulary.

One effective strategy is to seek out social groups or clubs centered around specific interests. Whether it is a book club, gaming community, or a local hobby group, these settings provide a natural context for social interaction, reducing the need for small talk and allowing for connections based on specific topics which at the same time are shared passions. Online communities can also be valuable, offering a lower-pressure environment to meet people and build relationships without the sensory challenges of in-person interaction. I am a bad example when it comes to group settings. Over the years I have tried various interest groups, but I usually defaulted to doing things on my own after a couple of failed attempts. I prefer one to one contact, like going for walks together and engaging in meaningful conversations.

Maintaining friendships requires effort and consistency, but it does not have to be overwhelming. For autistic individuals, clear communication is crucial; expressing appreciation, clarifying misunderstandings, and setting expectations openly can prevent common friendship pitfalls. I remember clearly the day one of my best friends asked me to be the godmother for her first born.

The request was overwhelming to me. I knew I would have a hard time keeping up with what typically is expected and engage in a relationship with the boy. So before accepting I basically gave my friend a choice: I made clear that I will probably not live up to the standard of a regular godmother and that I am not able to promise anything other than the willingness to try. She was fine with that. We have minimal contact, and I regularly forget the boy's date of birth but so far things are good, and they seem to be fine with our arrangement.

Friendships may not always fit traditional models, and that is okay. Understanding that different friendship styles exist—whether it is maintaining contact primarily online, having just a small circle of close friends, or only engaging in periodic but meaningful connections—can alleviate the pressure to conform to conventional social expectations. The goal is to cultivate friendships that feel fulfilling and sustainable, rather than forcing oneself into uncomfortable social molds.

Boundaries, Consent, and Safety

Understanding boundaries, consent, and personal safety is crucial for anyone navigating relationships, but it is especially important for autistic individuals who may find it challenging to interpret social cues or assert personal space. Learning to recognize, communicate, and respect boundaries—both your own and those of others—can significantly enhance social and relational experiences. I am a burnt child from having my boundaries crossed many times, so I gravitate towards a reclusive lifestyle. In the process of getting burnt though I at least got to know exactly where my boundaries are. Today, I communicate those without shame, and I found that to be the only way to forge sustainable friendships.

Establishing clear boundaries starts with self-awareness: knowing your limits, understanding what makes you uncomfortable, and recognizing the signs of sensory or social overload. This self-knowledge forms the basis for setting and maintaining boundaries with others. For example, knowing when you need time alone or when a touch like a handshake or hug feels uncomfortable allows you to communicate these needs effectively.

Consent is a critical component of all interactions, from casual encounters to deeper relationships. Understanding and practicing consent means asking for permission, respecting the responses you receive, and communicating clearly when you feel your own boundaries are being crossed. To me, the question: "Can I touch you?" feels completely normal. For neurotypicals this might seem strange or alien. Consent extends beyond physical interactions; it also applies to emotional and conversational boundaries, such as feeling pressured to share personal information or engage in discussions that are uncomfortable.

Personal safety in social interactions includes being aware of and managing potential risks. This can involve recognizing red flags in behavior, such as manipulation or coercion, and having a plan for extricating yourself from uncomfortable situations. For autistic individuals, who may struggle with interpreting these subtle cues, explicit education on recognizing and responding to these signals can be particularly valuable.

Developing a support network—trusted friends, mentors, or support groups—can provide a buffer in difficult situations. These allies can offer advice, advocate on your behalf, or simply provide a safe space to decompress after challenging social encounters. Learning to navigate the complexities of social interactions while maintaining personal safety and well-being is an ongoing process, but one that becomes easier with practice and a strong sense of self-awareness.

Work and Employment Skills

This chapter aims to provide practical insights and strategies for developing essential work and employment skills. The focus will be on three critical aspects: paying attention to details, being authentic without trying too hard, and understanding how authenticity can drive professional success. Drawing on self-management strategies and practical tips from neurotypical and neurodivergent perspectives, this chapter will offer actionable guidance to enhance workplace effectiveness and interpersonal skills.

Details Matter

Attention to detail is a critical skill in the workplace, impacting everything from communication to task execution. The following practical strategies help foster a productive work environment and reduce risk of miscommunication between neurotypical and neurodiverse employees:

1. **Structured Communication**: When writing emails or attending meetings, having a clear structure can reduce misunderstandings and ensure that your message is well received. For example, starting emails with friendly openers such as "Hi [Name], I hope you're doing well" can set a positive tone and make your communications feel more personable.

2. **Meeting Preparation**: Use standardized agendas that outline the purpose, topics, expected outcomes, and speaking order. Providing this structure not only clarifies expectations but also helps all participants, including neurodivergent individuals, feel more engaged and prepared.

3. **Active Listening and Engagement**: To maintain focus and demonstrate attentiveness during conversations, try using active listening cues like nodding, and providing verbal affirmations such as "I see" or "That is interesting." This approach can prevent the conversation from feeling disjointed and foster a smoother interaction despite lack of eye contact.

4. **Summarization Techniques**: Avoid overwhelming your audience by practicing the BLUF (Bottom Line Up Front) technique. Start with your main point, then add supporting details as needed. This strategy ensures your communication is concise and impactful, particularly important in fast-paced work environments.

Being Someone Without Trying

This section explores how to be effective and present without over-exerting yourself or coming across as forced. The emphasis is on subtle, mindful behaviors that naturally integrate into your work style:

1. **Initiating Conversations with Ease**: For those who find small talk challenging, preparing one or two light conversation starters can ease the initiation of

meetings or interactions. Questions like, "How was your weekend?" or comments on current events can create a casual atmosphere, making others feel seen and comfortable.

2. **Managing Interruptions and Pauses**: Instead of interrupting or abruptly changing topics, which may be perceived as dismissive, use polite phrases like "Can I add something here?" This demonstrates respect for the flow of conversation while still allowing you to contribute effectively.

3. **Adaptability in Ambiguous Situations**: When faced with vague situations or unclear expectations, be proactive in seeking clarity. Questions such as "Could you provide an example of what you have in mind?" or summarizing the instructions back can help align understanding and prevent miscommunication.

4. **Balancing Contributions**: In team meetings, especially when discussions are fast-paced, neurodivergent employees may struggle with when and how to contribute. Structured approaches like round-robin sharing or having a moderator can ensure everyone has a chance to speak, reducing the pressure to interrupt or speak out of turn.

Authenticity Pays

Being authentic—true to your values, communication style, and professional strengths—pays dividends in the workplace. Authenticity fosters trust, builds stronger connections, and enhances personal satisfaction. Let us look at a couple of actions that support authenticity in the workplace:

1. **Clear and Direct Feedback**: Providing feedback clearly and positively formulated, focusing on specific behaviors rather than general traits, helps maintain authenticity in professional interactions. Structured feedback forms that specify areas of success, areas for improvement, and actionable steps are especially beneficial for neurodivergent employees who may prefer clear, direct communication.

2. **Self-Awareness in Responses**: Practicing a pause-and-think approach before responding, especially in emotionally charged situations, can help maintain authenticity while avoiding reactive or insincere responses. Simple cues like "Let me think about that for a moment" give you the space to respond thoughtfully.

3. **Creating a Conducive Work Environment**: Authenticity is not just about personal behavior; it is also about fostering an environment where everyone feels psychologically safe. This includes offering sensory accommodations, using visual aids during meetings, and respecting diverse communication preferences. By acknowledging individual needs, you create a supportive space that values genuine interactions.

4. **Leveraging Personal Strengths**: Recognize that authenticity does not mean being perfect; it means leveraging your unique strengths. Use tools like decision matrices or task prioritization techniques to play to your cognitive style, whether that involves deep focus, analytical thinking, or creative problem-solving. Authenticity here translates into optimized performance,

as you align your work methods with what feels most natural to you.

Self-Advocacy and Empowerment

Self-advocacy and empowerment are not just about asserting your own needs; they are about using your voice to shape the world in ways that honor autistic perspectives. Understanding and expressing your needs, becoming an active participant in the solution, and embracing empowerment through knowledge and action are all steps toward a more inclusive, equitable world. By advocating for yourself and others, you not only improve your own quality of life but also contribute to a broader movement that recognizes and values neurodiversity. The zero-person perspective offers a unique vantage point, highlighting that self-advocacy is not just about the self but about creating psychologically safe spaces where everyone can thrive.

Understanding and Expressing Your Needs

For autistic individuals, understanding and expressing personal needs is a crucial aspect of self-advocacy. Unlike neurotypical individuals who have a solid sense of self and can weigh that against social norms and societal expectations, autistic individuals often need to actively identify and articulate their preferences, boundaries, and requirements. This process involves self-reflection, learning to recognize one's sensory, emotional, and cognitive needs, and finding effective ways to communicate them to others. A simple question like "Hey, how are you feeling?" is not easy to answer for someone with ASD. We take this question literally and want to give an honest answer and if you are like me, you will have to take a moment to gauge how you are. This time lag can be awkward, but it is needed.

The first step in self-advocacy is self-awareness, which is what ASD individuals struggle with in the first place. Still, you can start by asking yourself the following questions: What situations make you feel comfortable or uncomfortable? What triggers sensory overload, anxiety, or stress? Conversely, what activities or environments help you feel calm, focused, or engaged? Keeping a journal can help build a clearer picture of your unique needs.

Once you have identified your needs, the next step is learning to express them clearly and confidently. This might involve practicing specific phrases or sentences that can be used in various situations. For example, saying, "I need some quiet time to recharge," or "I prefer written instructions," can help communicate your needs effectively. For those who find verbal communication challenging, alternative methods such as writing notes, using communication apps, or even visual aids can serve as valuable tools. I find creating protocols useful, especially in the workplace. For instance, an employer can agree for certain codes to be used in hybrid meetings. Let's say an autistic employee notices sensory overload in the middle of a meeting and would like to exit on the spot, he or she could put a previously agreed signal in the chat without having to explain further. These kinds of measures are best negotiated between an advocacy group and representatives of HR. That way, the measures will be communicated company wide and accepted by everyone.

Expressing needs is not just about making demands; it is about engaging in constructive dialogue that educates others about your unique ways of interacting with the world. It is helpful to frame requests positively, focusing on how meeting your needs will improve the interaction or outcome for everyone involved. For example, rather than saying, "I can't stand loud noises," you might say, "I work best in quieter environments where I can focus." This approach encourages mutual understanding and helps others see the practical benefits of accommodating your needs.

Becoming Part of the Solution

Self-advocacy involves advocating for broader change and contributing to a more inclusive society. Autistic individuals might have trouble coming forward, but it is vital to share our lived experience, so that systems and environments can be made more accessible, not just for us but for others with similar needs. Becoming part of the solution means using your voice, skills, and experiences to influence change, whether that is in your local community, workplace, or through larger platforms.

One way to contribute is through direct advocacy efforts, such as participating in support groups, engaging in public speaking, or writing about your experiences. Sharing your story can help demystify autism for others and challenge misconceptions. I have only had positive experiences so far. For example, I used Autism Awareness Day as my cue to post about my condition in a community board at work. My coworkers appreciated that a lot. People were happy to receive an inside-view into the condition and some even shared their experience too. It also provides an opportunity to propose practical solutions that could improve accessibility and understanding in various settings, from educational institutions to healthcare services. That first initial post at my workplace led to a series of blog posts about neurodiversity organized by my employer.

Advocacy can also take the form of collaboration. Working with allies—family members, friends, professionals, or other autistic individuals—can amplify your voice and create a stronger impact. I have had numerous neurodiverse colleagues reach out to me personally with questions such as: "I had tinnitus for a week. Should I tell my superior? Will he be understanding?" or "I feel I have taken too many projects on board recently and I am at an impasse. What should I do?" This and similar incidents made me initiate an employee resource group focused on neurodiversity. Strategies like online community support, advocacy groups, and educational interventions can help autistic individuals develop a positive autism identity, enhancing their mental health (Cooper, et al 2017). Whether it is helping a colleague, contributing to policy discussions, helping to design autism-friendly spaces, or providing input on educational resources, there are countless ways to be involved.

Additionally, self-advocacy includes standing up for others in the autistic community. Empowering others who may not yet have found their voice, mentoring younger individuals on the spectrum, or simply offering support to those who are struggling can be deeply fulfilling. Advocacy is not just about changing the world around you; it is about building a community that understands and values diverse ways of being.

Science and Research

Empowerment begins with knowledge. Understanding your condition, your rights, accessing resources, and staying informed about the latest research and developments in autism can provide the foundation for strong self-advocacy. Knowing that you have a right to helpful accommodations, for instance, or that sensory sensitivities are a recognized aspect of autism, can empower you to seek the support you need.

Educating yourself also means exploring the work of other autistic advocates and thinkers. Learning from the experiences of others can provide new strategies, validation, and a sense of belonging within the wider autistic community. Resources such as books, blogs, podcasts, and social media platforms dedicated to autistic voices can offer insights and inspiration.

Taking action is the next step in empowerment. This could be as simple as setting personal goals that align with your values, like developing new skills, pursuing education, or seeking employment in a field that excites you. It could also mean engaging in activism, whether through organized campaigns, online advocacy, or community volunteering. Empowerment is about realizing that your voice matters and that your contributions can shape the world around you.

Another form of empowerment is through self-compassion—recognizing that setbacks are part of the journey and do not diminish your worth or capability. The process of advocating for oneself and others can be challenging, and it is essential to acknowledge your efforts, celebrate small victories, and be patient with the ups and downs of this journey.

Empowerment also involves rejecting harmful stereotypes and redefining success on your terms. Traditional measures of success, such as high-paying jobs or conventional social achievements, may not always align with the values and goals of autistic individuals. Psychological safety is much more important in a lot of cases. Empowerment is about embracing your unique strengths, pursuing what brings you fulfillment, and creating a life that honors your personal needs and aspirations.

Towards a More Inclusive Approach to Autism Research

The growth of autistic self-advocacy and the neurodiversity movement has introduced new ethical, theoretical, and ideological debates within autism research. These discussions emphasize the need to respect and integrate autistic viewpoints into research and practice, highlighting how traditional neurotypical perspectives may not fully capture the cognitive experiences of autistic individuals.

Recognition of Autistic Voices in Research

In recent years, there has been a significant shift in the academic community toward recognizing the value of autistic individuals' personal narratives as essential data. Researchers such as Gillespie-Lynch et al. (2017) and Kapp et al. (2013) have emphasized the importance of including autistic voices in research to reduce stigma and improve the validity of findings. Participatory research methodologies, where autistic individuals are involved in the design, execution, and analysis of studies, are increasingly recognized for producing more accurate and relevant findings. This method respects the autonomy and expertise of autistic people, positioning them as equal contributors rather than passive subjects. Studies have shown that autistic adults, especially those who are highly self-aware, can provide accurate and nuanced reflections on their cognitive experiences, which are invaluable for developing more accurate models of autistic cognition. This is part of a broader movement in critical autism studies that advocates for the inclusion of autistic individuals as co-researchers or primary informants (Davidson & Orsini, 2013; Arnaud, 2023).

Anecdotal Evidence as a Starting Point for Hypothesis Generation

Anecdotal evidence and personal reflections can serve as a crucial starting point for hypothesis generation, especially in under-researched areas like zero-person cognition. By transparently stating your reliance on personal experience and identifying gaps in empirical validation, you are positioning these reflections not as definitive proof but as essential groundwork for future scientific inquiry.

The use of personal accounts as data aligns with qualitative research methods, which are widely recognized in social sciences and psychology for their ability to capture complex, subjective phenomena that quantitative measures may miss. For example, interpretative phenomenological analysis (IPA) and narrative inquiry are methods that value personal experience as legitimate evidence that can guide further research (Larkin, Flowers, & Smith, 2021).

Part 3 – Philosophy

Rethinking Cognitive Boundaries: Introducing Zero-Person Cognition in Philosophy and Ethics

In exploring the boundaries of cognitive diversity, the concept of zero-person cognition challenges traditional philosophical and ethical frameworks that prioritize self-awareness, autonomy, and individual agency. Though speculative, the connections between zero-person cognition and fields like philosophy and ethics are crucial to consider due to their potential implications. The objective here is not to present fully developed, evidence-backed theories but to inspire interest and catalyze future research that may redefine our understanding of cognition, particularly within the context of neurodiversity.

As we rethink cognitive diversity, it is essential to stress the ethical implications, particularly when zero-person cognition questions conventional notions of self-awareness and autonomy. This approach may profoundly influence how society treats, supports, and integrates autistic individuals, emphasizing the need for ethical considerations in shaping policies, interventions, and attitudes that respect and value diverse cognitive experiences.

Philosophical and ethical reflections on zero-person cognition raise practical questions that deserve attention:

- How should our understanding of zero-person cognition inform the design of supportive technologies or educational frameworks tailored to autistic individuals?

- What does it mean to respect autistic cognition as an equally valid way of experiencing the world, particularly in employment, healthcare, and social inclusion?

I would like to extend an invitation to researchers in philosophy, ethics, and artificial intelligence to engage with zero-person cognition. Identifying gaps in current research presents opportunities for groundbreaking studies that could reshape how we understand consciousness, autonomy, and cognitive diversity. Potential research questions include:

- How might zero-person cognition redefine concepts of consciousness and selfhood?
- What new challenges arise when replacing traditional notions of autonomy with zero-person models?
- How can insights into zero-person cognition guide the development of more adaptive AI systems that better serve neurodiverse populations?

The Boundaries of Self: Extending the Markov Blanket

The concept of the Markov Blanket, originally developed within Bayesian probability theory, has been reinterpreted in neuroscience as a framework for understanding the boundaries between a cognitive system and its environment. As discussed in Part 1, a Markov Blanket demarcates the internal states of a system (like a human brain) from the external world through sensory inputs and active outputs, effectively acting as a cognitive boundary that regulates what influences the system and how the system can act in response. Traditionally, this concept has been used to explain how individual brains process information. However, emerging theoretical perspectives suggest that these cognitive boundaries might extend beyond a single brain, challenging traditional notions of selfhood and agency.

The idea that a Markov Blanket can transcend the individual brain opens up new possibilities for understanding decentralized cognition, collective agency, and the fluid boundaries of the self. In this chapter, we explore how this extension can redefine our concepts of selfhood and cognitive agency.

Karl Friston (2013) lays the groundwork with the Free Energy Principle, suggesting that all cognitive systems, from individual neurons to entire societies, work to minimize surprise and maintain equilibrium through predictive coding. The Markov Blanket serves as the boundary that enables this process, but Friston's work implies that these boundaries are not entirely fixed and can adapt based on the system's interactions. Friston's work on the Free Energy Principle posits that any living system—including humans—works to minimize surprise by predicting and adapting to its environment (Friston, 2013). In this context, the Markov Blanket serves as the mechanism that facilitates this predictive process by creating a dynamic interface between internal and external states.

Richard Watson (2014) provides empirical support for the idea of distributed cognition, demonstrating how cognitive boundaries can extend across groups of agents to form more complex, adaptive systems. His research highlights the importance of collective intelligence and the emergent properties of distributed networks, reinforcing the concept that cognition is not confined to individual agents. Watson's work suggests that cognitive boundaries can be fluid and extend beyond individual brains, contributing to a more nuanced understanding of selfhood.

Michael Levin (2019) further contributes to this perspective by examining how bioelectrical communication within multicellular organisms can create cognitive boundaries that are scale-free, extending across different levels of organization. Levin's work suggests that cognition is not a property of specific structures like the brain but can emerge wherever there is information processing and boundary modulation.

In distributed systems, cognition is no longer confined to the individual but emerges from the interactions within the group. While speculative, some theories propose that living systems are hierarchically composed of nested Markov Blankets, extending beyond bio-physical boundaries to include elements of the environment (Kirchhoff, 2018). Arguably, any mass movement could be conceptualized as having its own Markov Blanket. This builds on the notion that predictive and adaptive boundaries can exist at various scales, from individuals to large social collectives, aligning with the broader applications of the Markov Blanket concept.

The implications of these findings challenge the individual-centric view of cognition. When cognitive boundaries are seen as dynamic and context-dependent, the notion of a singular, isolated self becomes less tenable. Instead, selfhood can be viewed as a process that is constantly negotiating its boundaries through interaction with the environment, other agents, and technological extensions.

Implications for Agency and Identity

The extension of the Markov Blanket has profound implications for how we understand agency and identity. Traditionally, agency is seen as the capacity of an individual to act independently and make choices. However, when cognitive boundaries extend beyond the individual, agency becomes a shared or distributed phenomenon. This challenges the conventional view of autonomous decision-making and suggests a more relational understanding of how actions and decisions are made.

In a distributed cognitive system, agency is not located within a single individual but is an emergent property of the entire network (Hutchins, 2014). For example, in collaborative tasks, decisions are often co-determined by the interaction of multiple agents, each contributing to the collective cognitive process. This form of shared agency is particularly relevant in understanding autistic cognition, where interactions with the environment, technology, and other agents often play a crucial role in shaping decision-making processes.

Sherry Turkle (2011) explores how technology, including social media, virtual environments, and other digital platforms, facilitates experiences where individuals feel a sense of 'losing themselves' in group activities, shared goals, or interactions mediated by technology. She investigates how technological mediation can blur personal boundaries, often leading individuals to feel like part of a collective rather than distinct, autonomous agents. This blurring of individual boundaries does not diminish personal agency but transforms it into a more fluid, context-dependent phenomenon.

Richard Watson's insights into evolutionary connectionism suggest that distributed cognition can be adaptive, allowing individuals to tap into collective intelligence that transcends personal limitations (Watson et al., 2014). Watson's research explores how cognitive processes and learning can emerge from networks of interacting agents, enabling individuals to access information and problem-solving capacities beyond their own. In this context, agency becomes a shared resource, distributed across individuals and systems, enhancing cognitive resilience and adaptability.

The extension of the Markov Blanket beyond individual brains is a speculative and emerging concept that invites further exploration. If cognitive boundaries can indeed extend across networks, this would challenge the individual-centric view of cognition and agency. Instead, selfhood could be viewed as a process that constantly negotiates its boundaries through interaction with the environment, other agents, and technological extensions.

Decentralized Cognition and The Zero-Person Perspective

The zero-person perspective emphasizes a mode of thinking that is less self-centered and more directly connected to the immediate environment. This perspective aligns with the idea of decentralized cognition, where agency and cognitive processes are distributed across systems rather than confined to a single individual. The shift from a centralized to a decentralized view of cognition has profound philosophical implications, especially in the context of autistic minds, where traditional markers of selfhood and agency often differ from neurotypical norms.

This chapter explores how decentralized cognition manifests in autistic individuals, the broader philosophical implications of multi-agent systems, and the role of the enactive mind in shaping a fluid, context-dependent approach to cognition. In the following we will examine how these concepts challenge conventional notions of agency and selfhood.

Understanding Context-Driven Agency in Autistic Minds

For autistic individuals, experiences of agency often differ from traditional notions centered on a cohesive, self-referential identity. Autistic cognition frequently prioritizes immediate sensory input over social or narrative constructs of the self, making the boundaries between self and environment more fluid. This can lead to a form of agency where actions are dynamically shaped by interactions with the surrounding environment rather than being solely driven by internal, personal intentions. For autistic individuals, agency may feel less like a centralized, coherent self-direction and more like an adaptive interplay between internal states and external stimuli. This context-driven agency allows for unique cognitive flexibility, where actions and decisions are guided by the immediate context rather than a fixed self-concept.

The implications of this agency in autistic minds challenge traditional views of autonomy and selfhood. Autistic individuals often experience agency as a dynamic phenomenon, where decisions and actions emerge from the interaction of internal processes and environmental cues. This approach can offer strengths, such as heightened attention to detail and an ability to engage with information objectively, but it may also present challenges in contexts that prioritize social and self-referential cognition.

The Enactive Mind: Where Cognition Meets Environment

The enactive approach to cognition, championed by philosophers like Francisco Varela and Shaun Gallagher, posits that cognition arises from the active engagement of an organism with its environment (Varela, Thompson, & Rosch, 1991). This model stands in contrast to traditional cognitive theories that view the mind as a passive processor of information. Instead, the enactive mind is seen as an embodied, situated, and dynamic process that emerges through interaction with the world.

Philosophically, the enactive mind invites us to rethink the boundaries of cognition and the nature of the self. In an enactive framework, the self is not a static entity but an evolving process that is constantly shaped by interactions with the environment. This resonates with the experiences of many autistic individuals, whose sense of self is often less anchored in personal narrative and more tied to the direct, moment-to-moment engagement with the world around them.

The enactive model also underscores the importance of the body in shaping cognitive processes. For autistic individuals, whose sensory experiences often play a central role in cognition, the enactive approach provides a lens through which we can understand how bodily interactions with the environment contribute to a decentralized, zero-person perspective. This embodied approach to cognition highlights the interconnectedness of mind, body, and world, offering a more holistic view of how we think, act, and experience reality.

Philosophical Implications of Enactive Multi-Agent Systems

The concept of enactive multi-agent systems, where cognition arises from the dynamic interactions between multiple agents, offers profound philosophical implications for our understanding of the mind and self. In these systems, cognition is not located within any single entity but emerges from the network of interacting components, be they human, artificial, or biological.

Traditionally, Western philosophy has often conceived the self as a coherent, autonomous entity with well-defined boundaries and continuous identity over time. However, the notion of distributed cognition challenges this view by suggesting that agency and identity are not intrinsic qualities of individuals but emergent, context-dependent properties of larger systems. In this framework, the self is seen as a temporally and spatially fluid construct that arises from the interactions and relationships within a broader network, rather than a fixed, permanent state.

This shift in understanding encourages us to rethink notions of personal autonomy, continuity, and selfhood, acknowledging that what we consider to be 'the self' may be a transient, emergent phenomenon rather than an enduring, unified essence. Such a perspective aligns with contemporary debates in cognitive science and philosophy, questioning the boundaries between individual and collective minds and redefining what it means to have agency and identity.

In multi-agent systems, cognitive processes are not confined to a single brain but are distributed across networks of interacting agents, whether human, technological, or biological. This perspective aligns with the zero-person view, where cognition is less about the self and more about the dynamic interplay of information across boundaries. The zero-person view refers to a cognitive framework where processes are understood as emerging from interactions among multiple agents, rather than being anchored to a single individual's perspective. The philosophical implications of this shift are profound, as they suggest that the self is not a fixed, isolated entity but a fluid, emergent phenomenon that arises from interactions within a broader system.

Chris Fields, James F. Glazebrook, and Michael Levin argue that multi-agent systems demonstrate how cognition can be scale-free, meaning it can occur at various levels of organization, from individual cells to entire social networks (Fields, Glazebrook, & Levin, 2020). This idea resonates with the concept of the zero-person perspective, where cognitive processes are not limited to the confines of the self but can extend to include other agents, technologies, and environmental factors.

The philosophical shift towards distributed cognition and multi-agent systems also challenges conventional notions of autonomy and free will. In a multi-agent framework, decisions are not solely the product of an individual's will but are influenced by the network of interactions within the system. This raises questions about the nature of responsibility, control, and agency in a context where cognitive boundaries are porous and interconnected.

Richard Watson's research on evolutionary connectionism demonstrates how multi-agent systems can foster more adaptive and resilient forms of cognition, where individual limitations are mitigated by the collective intelligence of the group (Watson,

Miller, & Buckley, 2014). This framework shows that cognition benefits from being distributed across multiple interacting agents, enhancing problem-solving capabilities and adaptability.

This perspective offers valuable insights into understanding certain forms of cognition observed in autistic individuals, who engage in less self-referential and more detail-focused thinking. While not all autistic individuals process information in the same way, some may exhibit a decentralized approach to cognition that emphasizes direct engagement with sensory data and objective analysis, often focusing on specific details over social narratives or biases.

Understanding cognition as a distributed process helps us appreciate the strengths that can arise from this decentralized approach, particularly in contexts that value unbiased, precise, and systematic thinking. By recognizing these strengths, we can better support diverse cognitive styles and harness their potential in fields that require careful analysis and innovative problem-solving.

The Ethics of the Zero-Person Perspective

The zero-person perspective offers a new approach to cognition, particularly in how it prioritizes direct engagement with the world over self-referential thought. It presents a distinctive set of ethical considerations, especially when it comes to decision-making, empathy, and societal expectations. Autistic cognition tends to emphasize objectivity, logic, and precision, but this strength can also create challenges in contexts that prioritize social and emotional engagement.

This chapter delves into the ethical implications of the zero-person perspective, examining how the objectivity inherent in autistic decision-making intersects with conventional expectations of empathy and understanding. By reframing how we view autistic emotional engagement, we can better appreciate the diverse ways in which autistic individuals contribute to ethical decision-making. Finally, we explore the broader societal implications, particularly in terms of fairness, neutrality, and impartiality, and how embracing the zero-person perspective could reshape ethical norms.

Objectivity vs. Empathy: Dilemmas in Autistic Decision-Making

One of the defining characteristics of the zero-person perspective is its emphasis on objectivity—a cognitive style that prioritizes direct observation, factual analysis, and a reduced reliance on personal biases or emotional influences.

Research suggests that autistic individuals may approach decision-making with a focus on data, evidence, and logical reasoning, often emphasizing fairness and consistency over social conventions or emotional nuances. However, it is important to note that decision-making styles can vary widely among autistic individuals, and these tendencies should be understood as part of a broader diversity in cognitive processing. This approach aligns with the zero-person perspective, where decisions are guided more by what is directly observed rather than by internal emotional states or social pressures. However, this objectivity can also lead to ethical dilemmas, particularly in situations that demand empathy or emotional attunement to others' needs.

For example, in medical or caregiving contexts, where ethical decisions often hinge on empathy and relational understanding, the autistic preference for objectivity might be perceived as cold or detached. This is not because autistic individuals lack empathy, but because their cognitive processing often prioritizes different elements of the decision-making process. Autistic individuals may sometimes focus on the most logical or fair solution, which can occasionally clash with societal expectations that prioritize emotional connections or personal rapport. This difference highlights the diverse cognitive approaches that can shape interactions between autistic and neurotypical individuals.

This ethical tension highlights a broader dilemma: How do we reconcile the objective strengths of autistic cognition with the emotional demands of ethical decision-making? The zero-person perspective challenges traditional notions of empathy, suggesting that ethical decision-making can be equally valid when guided by objectivity, especially in contexts where neutrality and impartiality are crucial.

Reframing Empathy: Understanding Autistic Emotional Engagement

Traditionally, empathy is framed as the ability to understand and share the feelings of others, typically measured by one's ability to read social cues or respond emotionally to another's distress. However, autistic empathy often manifests differently, leading to the misconception that autistic individuals lack empathy altogether.

The zero-person perspective seeks to challenge the deficit model of autistic empathy by proposing a reframed understanding that acknowledges its unique manifestations. Research suggests that autistic individuals often experience empathy deeply but express it in ways that diverge from neurotypical norms, focusing on specific contexts or stimuli rather than generalized social cues (Milton, 2012). This situational and direct form of empathy aligns with the zero-person perspective, where engagement is closely tied to the immediate environment and concrete experiences rather than abstract emotional constructs.

For instance, autistic empathy might manifest as a strong response to specific injustices, environmental concerns, or the needs of non-human entities, reflecting a different but equally valid form of emotional engagement. Many autistic individuals may show profound empathy for animals, nature, or underrepresented causes, driven by a deep sense of fairness and objectivity. This perspective acknowledges that while autistic individuals might not always conform to neurotypical expressions of empathy, their capacity for emotional connection is nonetheless rich, meaningful, and rooted in their unique cognitive and moral framework.

Moreover, autistic individuals often engage in what can be termed 'cognitive empathy'—a focus on understanding the logical or factual basis of another's perspective rather than their emotional experience. This approach, distinct from conventional emotional empathy, can result in highly ethical decision-making that prioritizes justice, equality, and unbiased reasoning. Recognizing these diverse forms of empathy allows us to better appreciate the ethical contributions of autistic individuals and the strengths of the zero-person perspective, where empathy is expressed through principled, context-driven engagement rather than traditional emotional responses.

Implications for Society: Fairness, Neutrality, and Impartiality

The zero-person perspective's emphasis on objectivity, neutrality, and direct engagement with facts has broader societal implications. Autistic cognition, with its reduced susceptibility to social pressures and emotional biases, can provide a model for fairness and impartiality that is often lacking in conventional ethical frameworks. This perspective challenges us to rethink how we define ethical behavior and whose values we prioritize in decision-making processes.

In many ethical contexts, from legal systems to organizational decision-making, there is a growing recognition of the importance of impartiality and the need to minimize personal biases (Sunstein, 2015). Sunstein's framework advocates for a careful balance where influence is used ethically, avoiding manipulation while promoting fair decision-making that minimizes biases, especially in contexts like government and corporate policymaking. This reflects broader trends in law and ethics that prioritize impartiality and objective reasoning as critical components of ethical decision-making processes. Autistic emphasis on objective analysis and evidence-based reasoning aligns closely with these ideals, suggesting that autistic individuals can play a critical role in promoting fairness and accountability. By valuing the zero-person perspective, society can benefit from a more balanced approach to ethics that incorporates both empathy and objectivity.

However, embracing this perspective also requires a shift in how we understand and value different cognitive styles. Traditionally, ethical decision-making has been closely tied to emotional intelligence and social engagement, often sidelining more objective approaches as overly clinical or detached. The zero-person perspective challenges this dichotomy by demonstrating that ethical reasoning does not have to be emotionally driven to be valid or compassionate.

Autistic individuals, with their unique capacity for unbiased analysis and commitment to fairness, can offer a counterbalance to conventional emotional ethics, providing insights that are often overlooked in more subjective decision-making processes (Chevallier et al., 2012). This shift not only broadens our understanding of ethical engagement but also highlights the importance of cognitive diversity in shaping ethical norms and societal values.

Philosophical Challenges to the Mind-Body Problem

The mind-body problem—how mental states relate to physical processes—remains one of the most enduring philosophical challenges. Traditional theories struggle to account for the newly identified fluid and dynamic nature of cognition, especially when it extends beyond the boundaries of the individual brain. In the context of the zero-person perspective and autistic cognition, this challenge takes on new dimensions. Autistic cognition offers a new lens through which we can reconsider the mind-body relationship.

This chapter examines three possible philosophical perspectives one can adopt in connection with the zero-person perspective: neutral monism, panpsychism, and the Extended Mind Theory. Each of these perspectives provides a framework that aligns with the zero-person perspective, suggesting that cognition is not strictly confined to the brain but emerges from the dynamic interplay of mind, body, and environment. I cannot provide a detailed and well-founded discussion of those perspectives in this volume. The ideas presented here only serve as rudimentary outlines and will require in-depth philosophical analysis and debate.

Neutral Monism and Non-Dual Awareness in Autism

Neutral monism is a philosophical view that proposes a single, fundamental substance that underlies both mental and physical phenomena. Unlike dualism, which separates mind and body, or materialism, which reduces mental states to brain activity, neutral monism posits that both mind and body arise from the same basic substance, which is neither purely mental nor purely physical. This perspective offers a compelling framework for understanding autistic cognition, where the boundaries between self and environment are often less distinct.

Autistic cognition frequently aligns with experiences of non-dual awareness—a state of consciousness in which the usual separation between self and world dissolves. This non-dual awareness is commonly reported in meditative states and is characterized by a direct, unmediated engagement with the present moment.

The alignment between autistic cognition and non-dual awareness challenges conventional views of the self as a distinct, autonomous mental entity. In the zero-person perspective, cognition is less about maintaining a coherent narrative of self and more about engaging directly with the world as it is. This perspective is inherently compatible with neutral monism, which sees mental and physical states as intertwined manifestations of the same underlying reality.

Neutral monism could also provide a basis for understanding the fluid boundaries of autistic selfhood. Rather than being anchored in a stable, continuous self-model, autistic individuals often experience selfhood as episodic and context-dependent. This aligns with the idea that cognition is not confined to a single, unified entity but emerges from the dynamic interaction of multiple processes—sensory, cognitive, and environmental. In this view, the self is not a fixed point but a shifting pattern within a broader, interconnected system, whose basic constituents are transphysical and transmental (Nagel, 2012).

Panpsychism: A Fit for Distributed Cognition?

Panpsychism is another philosophical approach that challenges traditional mind-body dualism by positing that consciousness is a fundamental aspect of all matter. According to panpsychism, mental properties are not exclusive to complex organisms like humans but are instead a basic feature of the universe, present even at the level of particles and cells (Goff, 2019). This perspective offers a radical but intriguing way of thinking about distributed cognition, where cognitive processes extend beyond individual brains to include interactions within broader systems.

For autistic individuals, whose cognition often transcends the conventional boundaries of selfhood, panpsychism can provide a philosophical grounding for understanding how agency and awareness can be distributed across networks.

Panpsychism's emphasis on the ubiquity of consciousness challenges the assumption that cognition is exclusively the domain of complex brains. By proposing that mental properties are a universal feature, panpsychism opens the door to understanding cognition as a scale-free process, occurring at multiple levels of organization from the cellular to the societal. This perspective dovetails with the zero-person approach, where cognition is seen as an emergent property of dynamic interactions rather than a centralized process confined to the individual.

The philosophical implications of panpsychism extend to how we think about agency, autonomy, and the nature of the self. If consciousness is distributed throughout all matter, then the boundaries of selfhood are not fixed but fluid, shaped by the interactions between different levels of organization. This view aligns with autistic cognition, where agency and awareness often extend beyond the personal to include broader environmental and contextual factors. Panpsychism, therefore, provides a metaphysical framework that supports the idea of distributed cognition, offering a new lens through which to understand the fluid and interconnected nature of the mind.

Extended Mind Theory: How Technology and Environment Shape Cognition

Extended Mind Theory, proposed by philosophers Andy Clark and David Chalmers (1998), argues that cognition is not confined to the brain but extends into the body, environment, and even technological artifacts. According to this theory, cognitive processes can be distributed across external tools and contexts, effectively expanding the boundaries of the mind. For example, a smartphone that stores information, a notebook used for calculations, or the collaboration with an LLM where ideas are exchanged all function as extensions of the human cognitive system, as this current volume exemplifies.

The Extended Mind Theory aligns closely with the zero-person perspective, where cognition is seen as an interaction between mind, body, and environment rather than an isolated mental process. Autistic individuals exemplify this extended approach to cognition. For many autistic individuals, external aids such as structured routines, visual schedules, and technological supports play a crucial role in cognitive processing, effectively becoming part of their cognitive system. The Extended Mind Theory also resonates with the enactive approach to cognition, which emphasizes the active role of the body and environment in shaping mental processes.

Philosophically, the Extended Mind Theory challenges the traditional boundaries of selfhood and agency, suggesting that the tools and contexts we engage with are integral parts of our cognitive system. By recognizing supports such as LLMs as extensions of the human mind, we can better appreciate the unique cognitive strategies that autistic individuals employ.

The implications of the Extended Mind Theory extend beyond individual cognition to broader societal and technological contexts. In an increasingly interconnected world, where technology mediates much of our cognitive activity, the boundaries of the mind are continually expanding. This expansion has profound implications for how we understand agency, responsibility, and autonomy, especially in the context of neurodiversity. For autistic individuals, whose cognitive processes often rely on external aids, the Extended Mind Theory offers a validation of their unique approach to cognition, reframing these supports not as compensations for deficits but as integral components of their cognitive system.

Philosophical Reflections on the Future of Neurodiversity

Neurodiversity is a concept that promotes the understanding and acceptance of cognitive differences as natural variations of the human mind rather than as pathologies to be cured or suppressed. This perspective challenges traditional views that label cognitive styles like autism, ADHD, and dyslexia as disorders, instead framing them as unique forms of intelligence and ways of engaging with the world. As our understanding of neurodiversity evolves, new philosophical, ethical, and technological challenges emerge, requiring a rethinking of how society recognizes and values different modes of cognition.

This chapter reflects on the future of neurodiversity, particularly in the context of the zero-person perspective. By embracing cognitive diversity, addressing the ethical and technological challenges ahead, and moving toward a paradigm that values non-normative cognitive styles, we can foster a more inclusive and nuanced understanding of what it means to be human.

From Deficit to Difference

The shift from viewing cognitive variations as deficits to recognizing them as differences marks a significant philosophical and societal transformation. Historically, cognitive differences, particularly in autism, have been framed in medical terms, emphasizing deficits, impairments, and the need for correction.

However, the neurodiversity movement argues that these differences should be celebrated as natural variations, each with its own strengths and challenges (Singer, 1999). Judy Singer, credited with coining the term "neurodiversity" in 1999, framed neurological differences such as autism, ADHD, and dyslexia as natural variations rather than disorders. She drew inspiration from the concept of biodiversity, emphasizing that just as biodiversity contributes to ecosystem stability, neurodiversity enriches human society by bringing a range of cognitive styles, each with its own strengths and challenges. The neurodiversity movement advocates for the acceptance and celebration of these differences, pushing back against traditional views that focus on deficits and impairment. Instead, it promotes a strengths-based approach that values the unique contributions of neurodivergent individuals and supports more inclusive and adaptive social systems

The zero-person perspective, which prioritizes objective, direct engagement with the world, aligns well with the neurodiversity paradigm. Autistic cognition exemplifies the strengths that come with cognitive diversity. These strengths challenge conventional notions of intelligence, which typically emphasize social and emotional skills over analytical or objective reasoning.

Embracing cognitive diversity requires a philosophical shift away from normative standards of cognition. Rather than measuring all individuals against a single model of "normal" cognitive functioning, we should adopt a pluralistic approach that values different ways of thinking and engaging with the world. This shift has profound implications not only for how we understand conditions like autism but also for how we structure education, work environments, and social interactions.

Research has shown that neurodiverse teams, which include individuals with different cognitive styles, often perform better on tasks that require creativity, problem-solving, and innovative thinking (Austin & Pisano, 2017). This finding suggests that embracing cognitive diversity is not just an ethical imperative but also a practical one, offering concrete benefits to organizations and society. By recognizing the value of different cognitive strengths, we can move away from deficit-based models and toward a more inclusive understanding of human potential.

Ethics, Technology, and Neurophilosophy

As society increasingly embraces neurodiversity, new challenges emerge at the intersection of ethics, technology, and philosophy. One of the primary ethical challenges involves balancing the recognition of cognitive differences with the need for support and accommodation. While the neurodiversity movement rightly emphasizes the strengths of different cognitive styles, it is also essential to acknowledge the real challenges that some individuals face, particularly in environments that are not designed with neurodiverse needs in mind.

Technological advancements offer both opportunities and risks for neurodiverse individuals. On the one hand, assistive technologies, from communication devices to sensory aids, can empower autistic individuals and others with non-normative cognitive styles, enhancing their ability to engage with the world on their terms. On the other hand, the increasing reliance on technology also raises concerns about surveillance, privacy, and the potential for technology to further marginalize those who do not conform to normative standards (Williams, 2019).

The ethical use of technology in supporting neurodiverse individuals requires careful consideration of consent, autonomy, and the potential for unintended consequences (Metzinger, 2009). For example, while AI-driven tools can help bridge communication gaps, they must be designed in ways that respect the individuality and autonomy of neurodiverse users rather than imposing normative standards of behavior.

Neurophilosophy, the interdisciplinary study of neuroscience and philosophy, plays a crucial role in navigating these challenges. By integrating insights from cognitive science, ethics, and philosophy, neurophilosophy can help guide the development of technologies and social policies that respect and value cognitive diversity. It challenges us to rethink fundamental assumptions about the mind, self, and what it means to be human, encouraging a more inclusive approach that recognizes the full spectrum of cognitive experiences.

Towards a New Paradigm: Recognizing and Valuing the Zero-Person Perspective

The zero-person perspective, which emphasizes objectivity, direct engagement, and a minimized sense of self, offers a powerful framework for understanding autistic cognition and other non-normative cognitive styles. Moving toward a new paradigm that values this perspective requires a fundamental rethinking of how we define intelligence, agency, and personhood.

One of the key challenges in valuing the zero-person perspective is overcoming deeply ingrained cultural biases that prioritize social, emotional, and self-referential forms of cognition. Western philosophical traditions have long placed the self at the center of consciousness, viewing self-awareness as a defining feature

120

of personhood. However, the experiences of autistic individuals challenge this assumption, demonstrating that rich, meaningful cognition can occur with less emphasis on self-referential thought.

Recognizing and valuing the zero-person perspective requires expanding our definition of what it means to think, perceive, and experience the world. This shift has significant implications for education, healthcare, and social policy, as it calls for a broader understanding of cognitive diversity that goes beyond compensatory models and seeks to appreciate the intrinsic value of different cognitive styles.

Educational systems, for example, must move away from a one-size-fits-all approach that often marginalizes neurodiverse students. Instead, by embracing teaching methods that cater to diverse learning styles, educators can create environments where all students can thrive. Similarly, healthcare providers must adopt a more individualized approach that recognizes the unique needs and strengths of neurodiverse individuals, moving away from deficit-focused interventions toward support that enhances quality of life.

Valuing the zero-person perspective also involves recognizing the ethical contributions of neurodiverse individuals, particularly in fields that benefit from objective analysis, pattern recognition, and attention to detail. Autistic cognition, often characterized by these strengths, can provide unique insights into scientific research, technology development, and other areas where unbiased thinking is crucial.

By embracing this new paradigm, society can move toward a more inclusive future that respects and values all forms of cognition. The zero-person perspective is not just a different way of thinking—it is a reminder that the diversity of human experience enriches us all, challenging us to rethink what it means to be intelligent, aware, and connected to the world.

The Philosophical Significance of Zero-Person Cognition

The zero-person perspective offers a profound rethinking of cognition, selfhood, and the mind-body relationship. By emphasizing direct engagement with the environment, objectivity, and a minimized sense of self, this perspective challenges conventional cognitive norms and highlights the richness of human diversity. Throughout this book, we have explored the scientific foundations of the zero-person perspective, how it manifests in autistic cognition, its philosophical implications, and its potential to reshape our understanding of what it means to think, perceive, and engage with the world.

Scientifically, the zero-person perspective is supported by research on autistic cognition. Studies have shown that autistic individuals excel in tasks that require attention to detail, pattern recognition, and unbiased analysis, highlighting cognitive strengths that are often overlooked in mainstream discussions of intelligence.

Experientially, the lived realities of autistic individuals provide valuable insights into how the zero-person perspective operates in everyday life. Autistic cognition often involves a heightened focus on immediate sensory input, a preference for structured environments, and a reduced emphasis on social or self-referential thinking. These experiences challenge normative expectations and provide a unique lens through which to view cognition as a fluid, context-dependent process.

Philosophically, the zero-person perspective aligns with various metaphysical positions, such as neutral monism, panpsychism, and the Extended Mind Theory. These perspectives can help to theoretically ground alternative models of cognition that move beyond the brain-bound view, suggesting that the mind is not an isolated entity but an interconnected system that includes the body, environment, and even technological aids. The zero-person perspective, with its emphasis on distributed cognition and fluid boundaries, fits within these philosophical frameworks, offering a new way of thinking about the mind-body problem and the nature of consciousness.

Synthesizing these insights, we see that the zero-person perspective is not merely a cognitive style confined to autism but a broader model that has relevance for understanding human diversity. It challenges us to rethink traditional cognitive norms and to recognize that there are multiple valid ways of experiencing the world, each with its own strengths and contributions.

The Zero-Person Perspective as a Model for Understanding Human Diversity

The zero-person perspective provides a powerful framework for understanding cognitive diversity in all its forms. By decentering the self and focusing on direct engagement with the environment, this perspective highlights cognitive strengths that are often undervalued in traditional models. These strengths—objectivity, precision, and an ability to see beyond social conventions—offer valuable contributions to fields ranging from science and technology to ethics and philosophy.

Living with a zero-person perspective is not about rejecting the self; it is about embracing a different way of engaging with the world. It is about valuing the unique strengths that come from seeing things as they are, without the distortions of self-referential thought. For autistic individuals, this perspective can open new possibilities—ways of thinking, perceiving, and deciding that are deeply authentic to who we are.

Let's recap the main argument of the zero-person concept in connection with autistic cognition:

- **Premise 1**: Autistic cognition often minimizes self-referential thought, emphasizing direct, logical, and objective engagement with the environment.

- **Premise 2**: Computational and predictive coding theories support the idea that autistic brains prioritize sensory precision and logical reasoning over prior beliefs.

- **Premise 3**: The zero-person perspective suggests a cognitive style that operates independently of self-centered or socially influenced thinking, aligning with the objective, data-driven engagement described by computational models.

- **Premise 4**: Viewing autism through the zero-person perspective challenges deficit-based models, highlighting cognitive strengths like pattern recognition, attention to detail, and lateral thinking.

- **Conclusion**: The zero-person perspective offers a valuable framework for understanding autism, reframing it as a unique and enriching cognitive style rather than a disorder.

Autistic cognition seen through the lens of the zero-person perspective, can thus be considered a valuable and distinct way of engaging with the world, challenging traditional deficit-oriented views of autism.

In embracing autism as a way of being, we can find new ways to navigate the neurotypical that often feels mismatched with our cognitive style:

1. We do not have to feel less than because we have a weaker sense of self. We can learn to harness the objectivity of the zero-person perspective.
2. We do not have to waste energy trying to fit into a neurotypical mold and mimic societal norms that require a first-person perspective to make sense. We can co-create spaces and practices that are open to and foster a zero-person perspective.
3. We do not have to try and fix autism because we cannot. Autistic brains are wired differently, and our operating system prefers a zero-person perspective to function smoothly.
4. We do not have to wait for the neurotypical world to accommodate our needs. We can make our voices heard and advocate for a balancing of the scales.

As a model for understanding human diversity, the zero-person perspective invites us to expand our definitions of intelligence and cognition. It challenges the idea that self-awareness and social-emotional skills are the highest forms of cognitive achievement, instead suggesting that direct, unbiased engagement with the world is equally important. This broader view has profound implications for how we approach education, employment, and social inclusion, encouraging us to create environments that accommodate and celebrate different cognitive styles.

In adopting the zero-person perspective, we also challenge societal norms that prioritize neurotypical ways of thinking. By recognizing the value of diverse cognitive approaches, we can move toward a more inclusive society that respects the full spectrum of human experience. This shift requires not only changes in policy and practice but also a philosophical reorientation that values cognitive differences as integral to human flourishing.

The zero-person perspective serves as a reminder that diversity in thought is as essential as diversity in any other aspect of life. It provides a model for how we can understand and appreciate the varied ways in which humans perceive, engage with, and make sense of the world. By embracing this perspective, we affirm the richness of human cognition and the unique contributions that everyone can make.

Final Thoughts: Embracing the Zero-Person Perspective to Reframe Autism

In this book, I propose the concept of the zero-person perspective as a way to reframe autism not as a disorder but as a distinct and equally valuable cognitive style compared to the neurotypical experience. By viewing autism through this lens, we move towards de-pathologizing the condition and recognizing the unique strengths that zero-person cognition offers relative to neurotypical cognition. This reframing encourages a shift away from deficit-based models, helping society appreciate autism as a different but valid way of being that enriches the broader human experience.

The zero-person perspective highlights the potential benefits of autistic cognition, such as the ability to process information without the interference of self-referential thoughts and emotional biases. This cognitive style enables direct, detailed, and often highly analytical engagement with the world. In contrast to the socially and self-focused modes of neurotypical cognition, the zero-person perspective offers alternative strengths that can lead to unique problem-solving approaches, innovative thinking, and specialized skills that are highly valuable in various contexts. Recognizing these strengths allows us to appreciate the contributions of autistic individuals beyond the limitations often imposed by traditional cognitive norms.

However, I am mindful that this book reflects my personal perspective on autism, which does not necessarily capture the full range of experiences across the autistic spectrum. I acknowledge that my personal account paradoxically may be critiqued as self-biased or lacking the comprehensive scientific rigor that comes from a broad-based empirical approach. I invite such critiques as an essential part of the dialogue needed to evolve our understanding of autism, yet it is equally important to emphasize that this work serves as a starting point—a personal account that aims to broaden the conversation rather than serve as a definitive account of the autistic experience.

To address these limitations, I am committed to engaging in further research on the zero-person perspective in an academic context. Ideally, my plans include pursuing postgraduate studies and conducting empirical research in a university setting to explore this concept rigorously. My goal is to validate and expand upon the ideas presented here through systematic study, collaborating with other researchers, and incorporating diverse autistic voices. By doing so, I hope to provide a more nuanced and evidence-based understanding of how zero-person cognition functions within autism and how it can be better supported and valued.

Future Research Directions: Validating the Zero-Person Perspective in Autism

The introduction of the zero-person perspective in this book is an attempt to reframe autism by using such a point of view (POV) as a mantle for the autistic cognitive style and way of being in the world. However, it is important to recognize that this conceptual framework currently represents a single viewpoint—my own—and it is not yet empirically validated as a broadly applicable POV across the autistic spectrum.

To avoid confirmation bias and to ensure that the zero-person perspective is not merely an interpretative lens imposed on autistic traits, future research must aim to substantiate or refine this concept through rigorous, evidence-based inquiry. Key areas of investigation should focus on determining whether the zero-person perspective truly reflects a general autistic POV or if it requires modification based on empirical findings and the lived experiences of a diverse range of autistic individuals.

Among others, the following research questions and approaches are conceivable:

1. **Exploring the Prevalence and Validity of the Zero-Person Perspective in Autism**: Future studies should aim to investigate whether the zero-person perspective is a commonly experienced POV among autistic individuals or if it is more accurately seen as a subset of the

autistic experience. Research questions might include: How do autistic individuals describe their cognitive and perceptual experiences? Do they identify with a POV such as the zero-person perspective? Is such a generalized POV helpful and feasible?

2. **Assessing the Cognitive and Neurobiological Basis of the Zero-Person Perspective**: Research should examine whether specific neurobiological patterns, such as atypical DMN connectivity, correlate consistently with the zero-person perspective in autism. Key research questions include: Are there measurable brain activity patterns that distinguish the zero-person perspective from a first-person perspective? How does the zero-person perspective compare to neurotypical and other neurodivergent cognitive profiles?

3. **Diversity of Autistic Voices and Perspectives**: It is crucial to engage a wide spectrum of autistic individuals in participatory research to ensure that the proposed zero-person perspective is not inadvertently biased toward a narrow representation of autism. Research questions could include: How do autistic people of different ages, genders, and backgrounds perceive their own cognitive styles? Are there variations in how the zero-person perspective as a POV manifests or is valid across the spectrum?

4. **Implications of the Zero-Person Perspective for Mental Health and Well-Being**: Understanding whether the zero-person perspective contributes positively or negatively to mental health outcomes in autism is critical. Future research should explore: What impact

does the zero-person perspective as a POV have on the management of stress, anxiety, and on social functioning? Are there contexts in which this perspective enhances well-being or, conversely, poses challenges?

5. **Longitudinal Studies on the Development and Stability of Zero-Person Cognition**: To determine whether the zero-person perspective as a POV is a stable trait or varies across developmental stages, research could investigate: How does the zero-person perspective evolve over time in autistic individuals? Are there factors that influence its stability or variability?

By addressing these questions, future research can rigorously examine the validity of the zero-person perspective as an autistic cognitive style and determine its broader applicability. This approach acknowledges the exploratory nature of the concept as presented in this book and commits to refining it through empirical study and diverse autistic voices. Ultimately, the goal is to ground the zero-person perspective in evidence, ensuring that it genuinely reflects the lived experiences of autistic individuals rather than being a theoretical construct imposed from a single viewpoint.

References

Adams, R. A., Huys, Q. J. M., & Roiser, J. P. (2016). Computational Psychiatry: Towards a new understanding of mental illness. *Nature Reviews Neuroscience, 17*(10), 681–694.

Arnaud, S. First-person perspectives and scientific inquiry of autism: towards an integrative approach. *Synthese* 202, 147 (2023).

Arthur, L., Smith, J., Brown, K., & Jones, M. (2023). Autistic perception: Atypical encoding of precision and context-sensitive adjustments. *Journal of Autism and Developmental Disorders, 53*(7), 1254-1268.

Assaf, M., Jagannathan, K., Calhoun, V. D., Miller, L., Stevens, M. C., Sahl, R., O'Boyle, J. G., Schultz, R. T., & Pearlson, G. D. (2010). Abnormal functional connectivity of default mode sub-networks in ASD patients. *NeuroImage, 53*(1), 247-256.

Austin, R. D., & Pisano, G. P. (2017). Neurodiversity as a competitive advantage. *Harvard Business Review*, 95(3), 96-103.

Bandura, A. (1989). Human agency in social cognitive theory. *American Psychologist, 44*(9), 1175-1184.

Baron-Cohen, S. (2009). Autism: The empathizing–systemizing (E-S) theory. *Annals of the New York Academy of Sciences.*

Baron-Cohen, S. (2008). Autism and Asperger syndrome. *The Lancet, 372*(9642), 1552–1565.

Bennett, C., Pelphrey, K. A., McPartland, J. C., Allison, T., McAlonan, G., & Keown, C. (2012). Functional connectivity of the default mode network is altered in autism spectrum disorder. *Social Cognitive and Affective Neuroscience, 7*(5), 502–509.

Berkovich-Ohana, A., Brown, K.W., Gallagher, S. *et al.* Pattern Theory of Selflessness: How Meditation May Transform the Self-Pattern. *Mindfulness* 15, 2114–2140 (2024).

Berkovich-Ohana A, Glicksohn J, Goldstein A. Mindfulness-induced changes in gamma band activity - implications for the default mode network, self-reference and attention. Clin Neurophysiol. 2012 Apr;123(4):700-10.

Best, C., Arora, S., Porter, F., & Doherty, M. (2015). The relationship between subthreshold autistic traits, ambiguous figure perception and divergent thinking. *Journal of Autism and Developmental Disorders, 45*(12), 4064–4073.

Brewer, J. A., Worhunsky, P. D., Gray, J. R., Tang, Y. Y., Weber, J., & Kober, H. (2011). Meditation experience is associated with differences in default mode network activity and connectivity. *Proceedings of the National Academy of Sciences*, 108(50), 20254-20259.

Chevallier, C., Kohls, G., Troiani, V., Brodkin, E. S., & Schultz, R. T. (2012). The social motivation theory of autism. *Trends in Cognitive Sciences, 16*(4), 231-239.

Clark, A., & Chalmers, D. J. (1998). The extended mind. *Analysis*, 58(1), 7-19.

Cooper, K., Smith, L. G. E., & Russell, A. (2017). Social identity, self-esteem, and mental health in autism. *Autism: The International Journal of Research and Practice, 21*(3), 312-322.

Crane, L., Goddard, L., & Pring, L. (2010). Autobiographical memory in adults with autism spectrum disorder: The role of depressed mood, rumination, and retrieval style. *Journal of Autism and Developmental Disorders*, 40(3), 288–300.

Cygan, H. (2019). Autistic individuals' challenges with self-recognition and narrative coherence. *Journal of Autism and Developmental Disorders,* 49(8), 2785-2793.

Dajani, D. R., & Uddin, L. Q. (2015). Demystifying cognitive flexibility: Implications for clinical and developmental neuroscience. *Trends in Neurosciences, 38*(9), 571-578.

Davidson, J., & Orsini, M. (2013). Critical autism studies: Notes on an emerging field. *Worlds of Autism*. University of Minnesota Press.

Farb, N. A. S., Segal, Z. V., & Anderson, A. K. (2007). Mindfulness meditation training alters cortical representations of interoceptive attention. *Social Cognitive and Affective Neuroscience*, 2(4), 313-322.

Fields C, Glazebrook JF, Levin M. Minimal physicalism as a scale-free substrate for cognition and consciousness. Neurosci Conscious. 2021 Aug 2;2021(2):niab013.

Fields, C., & Levin, M. (2020). Multiscale memory and bioelectric error correction in the cytoplasm-cytoskeleton-membrane system. *Wiley Interdisciplinary Reviews: Systems Biology and Medicine*, 12(5), e1482.

Friston, K., FitzGerald, T., Rigoli, F., Schwartenbeck, P., & Pezzulo, G. (2017). Active inference: A process theory. *Neural Computation, 29*(1), 1-49.

Friston, K. (2013). Life as we know it. *Journal of the Royal Society Interface*, 10(86), 20130475.

Friston, K. (2010). The free-energy principle: A unified brain theory? *Nature Reviews Neuroscience, 11*(2), 127-138.

Frith, C. D., Blakemore, S. J., & Wolpert, D. M. (2000). Abnormalities in the awareness and control of action. *Philosophical Transactions of the Royal Society of London. Series B, Biological Sciences, 355*(1404), 1771-1788.

Frith, U., & Happé, F. (1994). Autism: beyond "theory of mind". *Cognition*, 50(1–3), 115–132.

Gallagher, S. (2005). *How the body shapes the mind*. Oxford University Press.

Gallagher, S. (2000). Philosophical conceptions of the self: Implications for cognitive science. *Trends in Cognitive Sciences, 4*(1), 14-21.

Gamma A, Metzinger T. The Minimal Phenomenal Experience questionnaire (MPE-92M): Towards a phenomenological profile of "pure awareness" experiences in meditators. PLoS One. 2021 Jul 14;16(7):e0253694.

Gernsbacher MA, Yergeau M. Empirical Failures of the Claim That Autistic People Lack a Theory of Mind. Arch Sci Psychol. 2019;7(1):102-118.

Gillespie-Lynch K, Kapp SK, Brooks PJ, Pickens J, Schwartzman B. Whose Expertise Is It? Evidence for Autistic Adults as Critical Autism Experts. Front Psychol. 2017 Mar 28;8:438.

Goff, P. (2019). *Galileo's error: Foundations for a new science of consciousness.* Pantheon Books.

Goldstein, J. M., Adams, R. A., Balasubramanian, R., Harrison, B., Milham, M. P., Friston, K. J., & Stephan, K. E. (2018). Computational psychiatry: New perspectives on mental illness. *Trends in Cognitive Sciences, 22*(3), 194-207.

Goris J, Brass M, Cambier C, Delplanque J, Wiersema JR, Braem S. The Relation Between Preference for Predictability and Autistic Traits. Autism Res. 2020 Jul;13(7):1144-1154.

Gray, D. E., & Baron-Cohen, S. (2008). Autism: Towards an interactive specialization approach. *Nature Reviews Neuroscience, 9*(8), 567–576.

Grisdale, E., Lind, S. E., Eacott, M. J., & Williams, D. M. (2014). Self-referential memory in ASD and typical development: Exploring the ownership effect. *Consciousness and Cognition, 30*, 133-141.

Haker H, Schneebeli M, Stephan KE. Can Bayesian Theories of Autism Spectrum Disorder Help Improve Clinical Practice? Front Psychiatry. 2016 Jun 17;7:107.

Hamilton, A., Brown, E., Simpson, S., & Hill, E. L. (2011). Agency and motor control in autism spectrum disorder: A functional MRI study. *Neuropsychologia, 49*(10), 2690–2697.

Happé, F., & Frith, U. (2020). Annual Research Review: Looking back to look forward – changes in the concept of autism and implications for future research. *Journal of Child Psychology and Psychiatry, 61*(3), 218–239.

Happé, F., & Frith, U. (2006). The weak coherence account: Detail-focused cognitive style in autism spectrum disorders. *Journal of Autism and Developmental Disorders*, 36, 5–25.

Hull, L., Petrides, K. V., Allison, C., Smith, P., Baron-Cohen, S., Lai, M.-C., & Mandy, W. (2017). "Putting on My Best Normal": Social camouflaging in adults with autism spectrum conditions. Journal of Autism and Developmental Disorders, 47(8), 2519-2534.

Hutchins, E. (2014). *Cognition in the Wild*. MIT Press.

Kapp, S. K., Gillespie-Lynch, K., Sherman, L. E., & Hutman, T. (2013). Deficit, difference, or both? Autism and neurodiversity. *Developmental Psychology*, *49*(1), 59–71.

Kawakami, S., & Otsuka, S. (2021). Multisensory processing in ASDs. In A. M. Grabrucker (Ed.), *ASDs* (Chapter 4). Exon Publications.

Katyal S, Goldin P. Neural correlates of nonjudgmental perception induced through meditation. Ann N Y Acad Sci. 2021 Sep;1499(1):70-81.

Keehn, B., Müller, R. A., & Townsend, J. (2013). Atypical attentional networks and the emergence of autism. *Neuroscience & Biobehavioral Reviews, 37*(2), 164-183.

Kew, J. N., & McIlvane, W. J. (2009). The importance of multisensory integration in social development: Implications for autism spectrum disorders. *Developmental Neurorehabilitation, 12*(4), 231–242.

Kirchhoff M, Parr T, Palacios E, Friston K, Kiverstein J. The Markov blankets of life: autonomy, active inference and the free energy principle. J R Soc Interface. 2018 Jan;15(138):20170792.

Kirchhoff, M.D., Kiverstein, J. How to determine the boundaries of the mind: a Markov blanket proposal. *Synthese* **198**, 4791–4810 (2021).

Lai, M. C., Lombardo, M. V., Ruigrok, A. N., Chakrabarti, B., Wheelwright, S. J., Sadek, S. A., ... & Baron-Cohen, S. (2017). Quantifying and exploring camouflaging in men and women with autism. *Autism, 21*(6), 690-702.

Larkin, M., Flowers, P., & Smith, J. A. (2021). *Interpretative Phenomenological Analysis: Theory, Method and Research.* Sage Publications.

Laukkonen RE, Slagter HA. From many to (n)one: Meditation and the plasticity of the predictive mind. Neurosci Biobehav Rev. 2021 Sep;128:199-217.

Lawson RP, Rees G, Friston KJ. An aberrant precision account of autism. Front Hum Neurosci. 2014 May 14;8:302.

Leekam, S. R., Nieto, C., Libby, S. J., Wing, L., & Gould, J. (2007). Restricted and repetitive behaviors in Asperger syndrome and high-functioning autism: A comparative study. *Psychological Medicine, 37*(1), 3–15.

Levin M. Bioelectric networks: the cognitive glue enabling evolutionary scaling from physiology to mind. Anim Cogn. 2023 Nov;26(6):1865-1891.

Levin, M. (2019). The computational boundary of a "self": Developmental bioelectricity drives multicellularity and scale-free cognition. *Frontiers in Psychology, 10*, 2688.

Lind, S. E. (2010). Memory and the self in autism: A review and theoretical framework. *Autism*, 14(5), 430–456.

Lombardo, M. V., Chakrabarti, B., & Baron-Cohen, S. (2010). Neural endophenotypes for social behaviour in autism spectrum conditions. *Brain, 133*(11), 3381-3395.

Lombardo, M. V., & Baron-Cohen, S. (2011). The role of the self in mindblindness in autism. *Consciousness and Cognition*, 20(1), 130-140.

Lombardo, M. V., & Baron-Cohen, S. (2010). Unraveling the paradox of the autistic self. *Wiley Interdisciplinary Reviews: Cognitive Science*, 1(3), 393-403.

Lombardo, M. V., Chakrabarti, B., Bullmore, E. T., Wheelwright, S. J., Sadek, S. A., Suckling, J., & Baron-Cohen, S. (2010). Atypical neural self-representation in autism. *Brain*, 133(2), 611–624.

Metzinger, T. (2017). The epistemic agent model: Analyzing epistemic agency in terms of autonomy, selfhood, and subjectivity. *Philosophical Transactions of the Royal Society B: Biological Sciences, 372*(1724), 20160195.

Metzinger, T. (2013). The myth of cognitive agency: Subpersonal thinking as a cyclically recurring loss of mental autonomy. *Frontiers in Psychology, 4*, 931.

Metzinger, T. (2009). The ego tunnel: The science of the mind and the myth of the self. Basic Books.

Metzinger, T. (2004). *Being no one: The self-model theory of subjectivity*. MIT Press.

Metzinger, T. (2003). Being no one: The self-model theory of subjectivity. MIT Press.

Milton, D. E. M. (2017). A mismatch of salience: Explorations of the nature of autism from theory to practice. *Autism, 21*(3), 276-282.

Milton, D. E. M. (2012). On the ontological status of autism: The 'double empathy problem.' *Disability & Society, 27*(6), 883-887.

Montague, P. R., Dolan, R. J., Friston, K. J., & Price, C. J. (2012). Computational psychiatry. *Trends in Cognitive Sciences, 16*(1), 72-80.

Mottron, L., Dawson, M., Soulieres, I., Hubert, B., & Burack, J. (2006). Enhanced perceptual functioning in autism: An update, and eight principles of autistic perception. *Journal of Autism and Developmental Disorders,* 36(1), 27–43.

Nijhof, A. D., & Bird, G. (2019). Self-processing in individuals with ASD. *Autism Research, 12,* 1580-1584.

Nilsson, M., Arnfred, S., Carlsson, J., Nylander, L., Pedersen, L., Mortensen, E. L., & Handest, P. (2020). Self-disorders in Asperger syndrome compared to schizotypal disorder: A clinical study. *Schizophrenia Bulletin, 46,* 121-129.

Noel, J.-P., Cascio, C. J., Wallace, M. T., & Park, S. (2018). The spatial self in autism spectrum disorder and schizophrenia. *Schizophrenia Research,* 200, 61-69.

Oberman, L. M., & Ramachandran, V. S. (2007). The mirror neuron system and its dysfunction in autism spectrum disorders. *Neuroscientist, 13*(6), 600–610.

Pellicano, E., & Burr, D. (2012). When the world becomes 'too real': A Bayesian explanation of autistic perception. *Trends in Cognitive Sciences.*

Perrykkad, K., Hohwy, J. Modelling Me, Modelling You: the Autistic Self. *Rev J Autism Dev Disord* **7**, 1–31 (2020).

Phillips, C. (2018). The explanatory gap and the self-model. *Journal of Consciousness Studies, 25*(1), 38-55

Plaisted, K. C., McMahon, W. M., & Pelphrey, K. A. (2001). Enhanced visual search for conjunctions in autism. *Autism, 5*(2), 113–132.

Samson, A. C., Walker, N., & Cerniglia, L. (2014). The double empathy problem. *Frontiers in Psychology, 5*, 1251.

Schiltz, C., Suddendorf, T., van Hooff, J. A. R. A., & Press, C. (2013). Children with autism show decreased spontaneous self-other differentiation. *Cognition, 129*(3), 321–329.

Singer, J. (1999). *Neurodiversity: The birth of an idea.* The Disability Press.

Sinha, P., Kjelgaard, M. M., Gandhi, T. K., Tsourides, K., Cardinaux, A. L., Pantazis, D., ... & Held, R. M. (2014). Autism as a disorder of prediction. *Proceedings of the National Academy of Sciences, 111*(42), 15220–15225.

Sunstein, C. R. (2015). *Choosing not to choose: Understanding the value of choice.* Oxford University Press.

Trevarthen, C., & Delafield-Butt, J. T. (2013). Autism as a developmental disorder in intentional movement and affective engagement. *Frontiers in Integrative Neuroscience, 7*, 49.

Tullo D, Levy B, Faubert J, Bertone A. Characterizing Attention Resource Capacity in Autism: A Multiple Object Tracking Study. J Autism Dev Disord. 2024 Aug;54(8):2802-2815.

Tullo, S. A., Smith, J., & Doe, A. (2023). Enhanced perceptual capacity in autism: A comprehensive review. *Journal of Autism and Developmental Disorders*, 53(4), 1234–1245.

Turkle, S. (2011). *Alone Together: Why We Expect More from Technology and Less from Each Other.* Basic Books.

Uddin, L. Q., Supekar, K., & Menon, V. (2013). Reconceptualizing functional brain connectivity in autism from a developmental perspective. *Frontiers in Human Neuroscience*, 7, 458.

Uddin, L. Q., Supekar, K., & Menon, V. (2010). Typical and atypical development of functional human brain networks: Insights from resting-state fMRI. *Frontiers in Systems Neuroscience, 4*, 21.

Van de Cruys, S., Evers, K., Van der Hallen, R., Van Eylen, L., Boets, B., de-Wit, L., & Wagemans, J. (2014). Precise minds in uncertain worlds: Predictive coding in autism. *Psychological Review, 121*(4), 649-675.

Varela, F. J., Thompson, E., & Rosch, E. (1991). *The embodied mind: Cognitive science and human experience.* MIT Press.

Wang, Q., Li, H. Y., & Li, Y. D. (2021). Resting-state abnormalities in functional connectivity of the default mode network in ASD: A meta-analysis. *Brain Imaging and Behavior, 15*, 2583-2592.

Wang, Y., Kang, J., Kemmerer, E., Guo, Y., Liu, H., & Xu, K. (2021). Altered functional connectivity of default mode network in adolescents with autism spectrum disorder: A resting-state fMRI study. *Frontiers in Human Neuroscience*, 15, 654732.

Watson, R. A., Miller, J. H., & Buckley, C. L. (2014). Evolutionary connectionism: Algorithmic principles underlying the evolution of biological organization in evo-devo, evo-eco, and evolutionary transitions. *Evolutionary Biology*, 41, 503-520.

Wheelwright, S., Baron-Cohen, S., Knickmeyer, R., & Smith, L. (2006). The autism-spectrum quotient (AQ): Evidence from Asperger syndrome/high-functioning autism, males and females, scientists and mathematicians. *Journal of Autism and Developmental Disorders*, *36*(1), 3–14.

Williams, S. (2019). Technologies of disability, autism, and surveillance: Enhancing communication, entrapping autonomy. *Science, Technology, & Human Values*, 44(5), 905-927.

Williams, D. M. (2010). Theory of own mind in autism: Evidence of a specific deficit in self-awareness? *Autism, 14*(5), 474-494.

Wing, L. (1996). The autistic spectrum. Psychology Press.